# Apply and Win
# Social Security
# Disability Benefits

Hayden M. Harris

Stay connected with developments in space tech; from satellite internet to space tourism, the final frontier is closer than ever.

Join a book club; discussions with others can offer diverse interpretations and insights.

Stay proactive in sharing your reading experiences; discussions, reviews, and recommendations enrich the literary community.

Stay vigilant about dental health; regular check-ups and good oral hygiene are essential.

# Introduction

Embark on a journey through the intricate process of obtaining Social Security Disability benefits with this detailed guide that demystifies the application and appeals procedure.

Discover the non-medical requirements crucial for securing Social Security Disability benefits. Explore the process from start to finish, understanding the steps involved and the nuances of each stage. Gain insight into requesting a hearing, preparing for it, and navigating the intricacies of the hearing process itself.

Learn what to expect after the hearing, and explore the subsequent steps, including engaging with the Appeals Council for further review if necessary. Dive deep into how the Social Security Administration (SSA) determines disability, understanding the Sequential Evaluation Process, which examines factors such as substantial gainful activity, severe impairment, and the Listings of Impairments.

Explore the crucial considerations of past relevant work and other work that could influence your eligibility for benefits. Delve into the complexities of different issues that may arise during your application journey, equipping you with a comprehensive understanding of the process.

Uncover the extensive Listings of Impairments, providing insights into specific medical conditions that could qualify for the Compassionate Allowances Program. Discover sample forms designed to assist treating doctors in accurately documenting your medical condition and supporting your application.

This guide serves as an invaluable resource, offering a comprehensive overview of the Social Security Disability application process. Whether you're just starting your application or navigating the appeals process, this guide equips you with the knowledge and understanding needed to successfully pursue the benefits you deserve.

# Contents

# PART I

# Non-Medical Requirements

# NON-MEDICAL REQUIREMENTS

Prior to even looking at the medical components of your application (the reason you can't work in the first place!), the Social Security Administration will look at certain non-medical requirements: age, insured status, and whether you have been engaging in "substantial gainful activity." You will also need to know what type of benefits you are seeking: Title 2 or Title 16.

## Age
To qualify for Disability benefits, you need to be ineligible, or not yet eligible, for retirement benefits; that is, you need to be under 69 years of age.

## Type of Benefits: Title 2 and Title 16
There are two types of Social Security Disability benefits. The first kind is called Title 2 by the Social Security Administration; the second kind is called Title 16 by the Social Security Administration.

When the Social Security Administration refers to these benefit programs, it is actually referring to the programs' legal titles under the Social Security Act. It is important to know which type of benefits you are seeking because Social Security will pay you back pay for Title 2 benefits, but not for Title 16 benefits. The requirements for proving that you are disabled are the exact same for either program.

### Title 2 – Social Security Disability Insurance (SSDI)
Title 2 benefits are benefits that you have to "pay into" – this happens usually by a payroll deduction. You may not have even noticed that this deduction was occurring. If you were paying attention, then you would have seen 15 cents for every Social Security tax dollar is put into the Social Security Trust Fund, rather than into the Social Security Retirement Trust Fund. That's an

interesting fact that may earn you some trivia points, but nothing that you need to know to win your benefits!

To qualify for Title 2 benefits, you need 20 out of 40 quarters of credits. One you have 20 out of 40 credits, you have "insured status." At this point, you are likely asking "what the heck does this even mean?" This means that you need to have worked for the last 5 out of 10 years.

*Insured Status*
Insured? Are they talking about whether I have medical insurance? No. The Social Security Administration does not care whether you have medical insurance. What they are talking about when the refer to being "insured" is whether you have "paid into" the system and earned 20 out of 40 credits. That's all.

So, if you switched jobs or were out of work for a period of time, as long as you had Social Security taxes deducted from your paycheck 5 years out of the last 10, you would qualify to apply for Title 2 benefits.

*Auxillary benefits*
If you qualify for Title 2 benefits, then your minor children and spouse may be eligible to receive a monthly check. These benefits to your family members are called "auxillary benefits." For your children to receive monthly benefits, your children have to be: under 18, an adult who was found to be disabled before he/she turned 22, or a high school student under 19. Your spouse can get monthly benefits if he/she is: 62 or older or has a child in their care who is under 16 or disabled.

The maximum benefit you can receive from Title 2 benefits is $2,788 in 2018 (it changes every year). The Social Security Administration uses a complicated formula to determine your *actual* benefit amount. I'm going to *try* and explain it!

First, they calculate your "covered earnings" – or those earnings that you paid Social Security taxes on. Then, they average your covered earnings over a period of years. This is called you average indexed monthly earnings, or AIME. From your AIME, they will apply a formula to calculate primary insurance amount, or your PIA. (Your PIA is a base figure that the Social Security Administration uses to set your benefit amount.)

This formula is fixed percentages for different levels of income to get different amounts that are added to come up with your PIA. So, for 2018, 90% of the first $895 of your AIME is added to your PIA plus 32% of your AIME from $885 to $5,397, plus 15% of your AIME over $5397. These amounts are added together and voila! That is your PIA. Confusing? I told you it was complicated!

Aside from crunching the numbers yourself, you can go to www.ssa.gov/mystatement to check your statement, or go to www.ssa.gov/planners/benefitcalculators.htm and calculate your benefit. A last option is to pop in to your local, friendly Social Security office and ask what your benefit amount would be.

*Title 16 Supplemental Security Income (SSI)*
Title 16 benefits are for people that did not "pay into" the system. People applying for benefits under Title 16 will need meet income requirements. That means that either you've never had income or your income when you were working didn't earn you any work credits because your income was low. Title 16 benefits are paid out of general funds, which is a different source than Title 2 benefits. Again, an interesting fact, but not one that you really need to know to win your benefits!

If you are applying for Title 16 benefits, you will have to complete paperwork listing your resources. Resources are: cash, bank accounts, land, vehicles, personal property, life insurance, and anything else you own that could be converted to cash to pay for food and shelter. All of your resources need to be less than $2,000 for an individual and $3,000 for a couple. If you are over $2,000 and would not qualify to apply for Title 2 benefits, you will, unfortunately, be out of luck.

Not only do you have to be under $2,000 for an individual and $3,000 for a couple, but you also need to be a citizen or a qualified non-citizen. A "qualified non-citizen" means that the Department of Homeland Security says that you are: a lawfully admitted permanent resident; have been granted conditional entry under the Immigration and Naturalization Act; paroled into the United States for at least 1 year; a refugee; granted asylum; deportation is being withheld; or a Cuban or Haitian entrant. You can also be considered to be a "qualified non-citizen" when you have sustained battery or extreme cruelty while in the United States. The important thing to note here is that *some* non-citizens can qualify for Title 16 benefits. If that is you, then be sure to gather your immigration documentation to submit with your application.

Some states will pay you a supplement, if you receive Title 16 benefits. In fact, every state except: Arizona, Mississippi, North Dakota, West Virginia, and the Northern Mariana Islands pays a supplement to disabled citizens who receive Title 16 benefits. The amounts range, with the highest state supplement being paid by California, who supplements with $910.72 in 2018. Some states have restrictions, for example, in Hawaii, you can only receive a state supplement when you are living in certain settings.

The Social Security Administration runs the state's supplements payment programs in the following states: California, Delaware, Hawaii, Iowa, Michigan, Montana, Nevada, New Jersey, Pennsylvania, Rhode Island, Vermont, and Washington D.C. That means that you will receive 1 check that includes your Title 16 benefit amount and your state supplement. If you live in a state other than those listed, you may have to apply separately in your state.

Remember, that states can change the supplement amount at any time and they can add restrictions.

One weird things about Title 16 benefits: you can't receive them if you live in Puerto Rico. Puerto Rico is considered "outside the United States." You must live in the 50 states, District of Columbia, or the Northern Mariana Islands to get Title 16 benefits (SSI). If this upsets you, please contact your Congressperson!

Here's a list of the differences between the two programs:

|  | Title 2 | Title 16 |
| --- | --- | --- |
|  | • Need to have insured status<br>• 5 month waiting period for first (5) months of disability<br>• Maximum of 12 months of retroactive pay<br>• paid out of the Social Security Trust Fund<br>• maximum monthly benefit of $2788<br>• eligible for auxillary benefits<br>• must meet definition of disability, as defined by SSA | • need to meet resource requirements<br>• citizenship requirements<br>• no waiting period<br>• no retroactive pay<br>• paid out of general funds<br>• monthly cap of $750, but most states have supplements<br>• must meet definition of disability, as defined by SSA |

Can you get both Title 2 and Title 16 benefits? Yes! Let's say when you were working, you earned work credits, but because your income was low, your benefit amount for Title 2 benefits is only $200. You would be eligible for Title 16 benefits in the amount of $550.

However, regardless of whether you "paid into" the system, the

Social Security Administration has exactly the same standards for deciding whether you are disabled.

**Substantial Gainful Activity**
This is a big one. To be eligible for disability benefits you must be *unable* to engage in substantial gainful activity. Yeah, but what IS "substantial gainful activity?" Well, the Social Security Administration has tacked a dollar amount to this term. In 2017, that amount was $1,170, unless you are blind, in which case that dollar amount is $1,950. In 2018, the amount is $1180, unless you are blind, then it is $1,970.

This number changes a little bit every year, as you can see.

So, if you are working and making over that amount per month, the Social Security Administration will deem you "not disabled" because you are engaging in substantial gainful employment. Your application will be denied before anyone even looks at your medical records because you don't meet the non-medical requirements.

Let's say that you can't make the salary that you were making before, but you are working a little – stringing together jobs or working part time to make ends meet. You aren't making even close to $1,180 and you applied and you were denied! What gives!

Here's the rub: the Social Security Administration can look at what you are doing for work – the physical and mental requirements) and determine from that that you *could* be making more than the dollar amount they determined to be substantial gainful activity.

Can you qualify for benefits while you are working making less than substantial gainful activity? Anything is possible, but this is a rare case, indeed.

# PART II

# The Process

# THE PROCESS

You met the non-medical requirements. What's next?

**Apply for Social Security Disability Benefits (Initial Application)**
The first step is to apply. You can go to your friendly local Social Security office, wait in line, and get the application there or you can call the Social Security Administration and they can take your application over the phone. Some attorneys will take your application over the phone as well. If any of these options aren't your style, you can apply online by yourself!

Go here: https://www.ssa.gov/applyfordisability/.

However you choose to apply, I would suggest that you gather the names, addresses, and phone numbers of your doctors. Also, you should know why you see each doctor. Having your doctors' names and contact information in one place will save you much time and hassle! I would also suggest having the names, dosages, and prescribing doctor of your medications in front of you as well when you apply.

Another list to compile is the titles of your past jobs and the physical requirements of each. "Past work" is defined by the Social Security Administration as any job that you've held within the last 15 years. If you've only had one job, then this part will be easy. If you've had many jobs, this part is a little more work.

Regardless of how many jobs you've had, the Social Security Administration will need to know: your job title, your job duties, how much you made per hour or per year, and what physical and mental activities were required of you in that job. Gather that information in advance and it will save you a little time.

*Onset Date*
Your onset date is that date that you became disabled. For a lot of

you, that is the day that you stopped working. It could also be the date of something significant, such as an accident or a surgery; something that happened and afterwards, there was no possible way you could work.

Your onset date becomes important because, if you are found disabled by the Social Security Administration, that is the date that they begin paying you benefits (for Title 16 benefits) or they begin the 5 month waiting period (for Title 2 benefits).

If you are having a hard time coming up with a date, it might help to talk to your doctor. There could be something revealing in your medical records that your doctor can point to.

## What Happens to My Application After I Apply?
Your application for Social Security Disability benefits is called your "Initial Application." Now that you've applied and your Initial Application is filed, be prepared to wait about 4 weeks. Why so long? A few things are happening.

First, your application is forwarded from the federal government at the Social Security Administration to a state agency. This state agency is referred to as the "Disability Determination Services" or DDS, for short.

Your "case" will be assigned to an examiner. This is the person that will be looking over your medical records and determining whether you are disabled. There are medical staff at DDS that will review your medical records and, if they find that there is insufficient medical information to determine whether you are disabled, they may make a doctor's appointment for you. This appointment is called a Consultative Examination.

*Consultative Examinations*
This appointment is of no cost to you and the doctor's report is forwarded directly to DDS. *Do not miss this appointment*. Do what you need to do to insure that you get to this appointment.

The doctor performing the exam will have been sent and perhaps have reviewed your medical records already. This appointment will most likely be brief and most clients tell me that the doctor didn't even do a comprehensive exam, and that the doctor didn't listen to their complaints. There's a reason for that: this appointment is not at all about *treating* you like your treating physician would. It is about assessing you.

*The Physical Consultative Examination*
The purpose of this exam is to give your examiner an opinion about what your physical limitations currently are. The examiner's job is to determine what your residual functional capacity is (much more on this later).

Big surprise: these doctors rarely find that someone has significant limitations. The best thing to do is to be honest about your limitations. The doctor will likely do some initial tests and then repeat some of the same tests later in the exam and you probably won't be aware that the doctor is doing that. If the doctor finds inconsistencies, if will appear as if you are not being 100% truthful. You don't want that! Don't be too vague and say things like "I can't do anything!"

You will probably be asked to give specific numbers about what you *can* do, so think beforehand about how long you can: sit, stand and walk; how much you can: lift and carry; and how often you need to change positions. Come prepared with the side effects of your medications. The doctor will also make note of your physical appearance, how cooperative you were, and even whether you were able to take you ID out of your wallet. Assume that you are being watched from the moment you enter the parking lot until you leave the parking lot!

Your residual functional capacity is a topic in and of itself, but, most basically, your residual functional capacity is what you can do now. Once DDS is finished reviewing your file, they will make a determination and send your file back to the Social Security Administration.

*Top 7 Tips for Your Physical Consultative Examination*
    (1)   Be on time or early
    (2)   Be honest about your limitations – don't exaggerate
    (3)   Put forth your best effort
    (4)   Be aware that the doctor or staff member will be watching you enter the office, walk into the exam room, get on the table, and leave in your car
    (5)   Be aware that the doctor will perform a test and later in the exam perform the same test and compare the results
    (6)   Be sure to mention all of your physical and psychological impairments
    (7)   Don't be vague about your limitations ("I can't do anything") and have specific examples of what you cannot do

At this point, be prepared to be denied, unless you are suffering from a terminal illness (more on that later). At this stage, close to 80% of initial applications are denied. **Do not give up if you are denied**!

*The Psychological Consultative Examination*
The purpose of this exam is to give your examiner an opinion about what your mental limitations currently are. The examiner's job is to determine what your residual functional capacity is (much more on this later). The psychological consultative examinations are much longer than the physical examinations.

The doctor will ask you questions about your history, and you will answer questions about your physical and mental impairments. The doctor will come up with a psychological diagnosis when he or she writes the report after your visit. The doctor will have been sent your medical records to review before your appointment, but don't assume that he or she has reviewed them beforehand. Sometimes, the doctor will give you some psychological tests. It is important that you put forth your best effort, since any inconsistencies in what you say or in the test results will not look good. To that end, don't intentionally miss questions or try and "play up" your symptoms. Whatever you are telling the doctor has to be supported by the medical records from your treating physicians.

Small details usually aren't problems, but big details are. Let me give you an example: you've been diagnosed with fibromyalgia and have suffered depression and anxiety as a result. You went in for a physical Consultative Exam and told that doctor that you haven't cooked a meal in years and that you haven't cleaned the house since Ronald Reagan was President! When you go for your psychological Consultative Exam, you tell the doctor that you have no trouble cooking and cleaning and, in fact, you do these things regularly but you can't leave the house. These are big inconsistencies that make it look like you aren't being 100% truthful.

Another example is when you tell the psychological Consultative Examiner that your memory is shot and you can't remember anything anyone tells you. When the doctor gives you a memory test (you won't know it's a memory test), you can actually remember almost everything. This is an inconsistency that, again, makes it appear as if you aren't being 100% truthful. Put forth your best effort and try to avoid these inconsistencies.

The doctor will be evaluating your ability to maintain concentration, attention, persistence, pace, and focus, and your ability to remember things, maintain attendance, and your ability to get along with others.

Think beforehand about when you were working. What kinds of difficulties did you have in these areas? Did you get fired? Did you lash out a co-workers? Did you miss so many days because of your pain that you were asked to resign? Jot down some specifics to tell the doctor.

Think about today. Can you cook? Can you follow a recipe? Can you finish a television show from start to finish and follow along without problems? Do you get lost when you are driving? Can you remember instructions that someone just told you? Do you go grocery shopping? Can you read a book? Do you spend any time on the computer? Do you isolate yourself? What kinds of things did you enjoy before that you can no longer do now? Jot down specific areas of difficulty to tell the doctor.

*Top 5 Tips for your Psychological Consultative Examination*
- (1) Be on time or Early
- (2) Be honest about your limitations – don't exaggerate
- (3) Put forth your best effort
- (4) The doctor should already have your medical records, but don't assume that the doctor has reviewed them
- (5) Think beforehand about your specific limitations

Just like the doctors who perform the physical Consultative Exams, the doctors who perform the psychological Consultative Exams rarely find that someone is significantly limited. The statistics show that you will be in that category, too.

At this point, be prepared to be denied, unless you are suffering from a terminal illness (more on that later). At this stage, close to 66% of initial applications are denied. **Do not give up if you are denied**!

# Reconsideration

If your claim is denied, you will get a denial letter that has a deadline to file your appeal. Do not miss this deadline. You can file your appeal by any of the methods that you used to file your initial application. This appeal is called Reconsideration. 10 areas of the country actually skip the Reconsideration step! Those places are: Alabama, Alaska, California (Los Angeles North and West branches only), Colorado, Louisiana, Michigan, Missouri, New Hampshire, New York, and Pennsylvania.

If you live in one of these areas, then you will still file an appeal, but your request will be for a Hearing, not for Reconsideration, so skip to the next section.

The appeal form will ask you what doctors you have seen since you initially applied, what medications you are taking, and whether anything has changed. Once you file your appeal with the Social Security Administration, your claim will be sent back to DDS. Your claim will be assigned to a different examiner.

At this stage, the examiner will look over your file and if anything has changed, the examiner will request updated medical records. At the Reconsideration stage, almost all claims are denied. In fact, in 2017, 87.2% of Reconsideration claims were denied!

You can think of it as the "rubber stamp" stage, as it is rare for DDS to reverse its determination. So, again, your claim is forwarded back to the Social Security Administration who will send you another denial letter.

At this point, you've gotten two denial letters. You still can't work, but the Social Security Administration is saying otherwise. It seems hopeless but please read this carefully: DO NOT GIVE UP. You are a fighter. How do I know? Having a chronic illness or an injury is incredibly difficult – you've had to endure doctor's appointment after doctor's appointment, test after test, some of you have been through surgeries, some of you were told that your condition is only going to get worse and you need medication to control pain (that you still feel, by the way); you've been through hell and you are still here. Don't give up now. Don't let the Social Security Administration tell you that you are not disabled when you know that you are; don't let them take away your hope.

# Request for Hearing

On your second denial letter, there will be a deadline to appeal. This appeal is called a Request for a Hearing before an Administrative Law Judge. Make sure that you file your appeal within that deadline. Once you file your appeal, your claim gets forwarded to the Office of Disability Adjudication and Review. At this point, be prepared to wait for quite a while. Your wait time depends on the office where it is assigned. In some offices, the wait times are 12-18 months.

This is enough time to have a baby, go out on maternity leave, and be back at work! This is an incredibly long time to wait, and my only advice is to be patient. Keep going to your doctors, keep taking your medications, and stay positive. After a hearing, the national average for claims being approved was around 54% in 2017. Much better odds than after your Initial Application or at the Reconsideration stage!

# The Hearing

You've waited and waited and finally you got a letter that tells you the time and place for your hearing. Most people want to know what they should wear. Wear something comfortable. Don't get dressed up. You want the judge to see you as you are on a daily basis. If it takes you 2 hours to get dressed up because you needed to rest several times, that isn't something that you are going to be doing on a daily basis. Also, if you can't tie your shoes and normally wear slide-type shoes, wear those. I would say most people wear something casual, like jeans. Some people wear sweatpants. It's all about what you are comfortable wearing and what is realistic, given your impairments!

Aside from what to wear, the first thing to know about your hearing is that it is "non-adversarial." It is supposed to be an "inquisitorial" proceeding. That means that no one from the Social Security Administration will be there arguing against your case! It is a different kind of experience than a trial in a courtroom. These are closed door hearings – no one from the public will be listening or watching. Most of the time, the hearing office is located in a federal building but don't be surprised if the hearing office you go to is in a strip mall or shopping center. Believe it or not, I have even been to hearings that were held in hotel rooms!

Many clients ask me: "do I have to go to a hearing? It sounds so intimidating." Yes, you must go. You may be nervous – you've never even seen a hearing before and there's a lot riding on it. I am going to describe the hearing in precise detail to let you know what to expect.

You will walk into a room with a judge sitting behind a slightly elevated desk; there will be three other tables in the room. One is for you and your representative; one is for the hearing recorder; and the last one is for a medical and/or vocational expert. There will be microphones that just look like black pads with a red light. Those microphones won't amplify your voice. Instead, the microphones are picking up your voice and the sounds in the room to make a recording that will later be filed and put with the rest of your case.

If you are having a hearing by video teleconference, everything will be the same except that the judge will appear on the television screen rather than at the slightly elevated desk.

The judge will likely greet you and your representative and ask you both to take a seat. The judge will start the hearing by asking you and any other witnesses (like a medical expert or a vocational expert) to raise your right hand and take an oath where you will swear to tell the truth under the penalty of perjury. Many times, the experts "appear" by telephone, which just means that they are on speakerphone. The judge will still ask them to raise their right hand, even though no one can see if they are actually raising their right hands.

After these preliminary measures, the judge may ask you some questions, or the judge may ask your representative to begin by asking you questions. If there is a medical expert in your case, the judge usually asks the medical expert to testify first to determine whether the judge can find you disabled at Step 3, which we will discuss later.

*Hearing Questions*
Your representative will likely have already asked you all of the questions she will be asking you in the hearing, so there will be no surprises. Luckily, there is nothing that you need to "study up" on. For all of these questions, you will easily know the answers. Below, I

have listed some of the questions that you are likely to be asked at your hearing. I have separated the questions into categories: foundational questions, job questions, impairment-related questions, functional questions, personal care questions, and social questions. Keep in mind that this isn't an exhaustive list and all of these questions may not apply at every hearing. These questions will give you an idea of what the judge will be interested in and what will be asked of you.

## Foundational questions

- What is your date of birth?
- How old does that make you?
- Where do you live?
- Do you live in a house, apartment, mobile home, etc.?
- Whom do you live with?
- Are you right handed or left handed?
- What is your current source of income?
- Have you ever received worker's compensation?
- How far did you go in school?
- Do you have any special training or licensing?
- Are you able to read and write in English?

## Job questions

- Are you currently working?
- What was the last job that you had?
- How long did you have that job?
- What were your job duties?
- Tell me about the physical requirements of the job.
- Was the job stressful?
- Did you have to work with a team?
- What sort of concentration was required?
- When did you stop working?

- ◦ Why did you stop working?
- ◦ Were you fired?
- ◦ Did you have lots of absences?

## Impairment-related questions

- ◦ What have you been diagnosed with?
- ◦ What makes you unable to work now?
- ◦ Do you experience pain?
- ◦ Where is the pain?
- ◦ On a typical day, what is your level pain on a scale of 1-10?
- ◦ Do medications help relieve the pain?
- ◦ What side effects do you experience as a result of your medication?
    - ◦ What have your doctors told you about your impairment?
    - ◦ Do you have good and bad days?
    - ◦ What can you do on a bad day?
    - ◦ How many bad days do you have per month?
    - ◦ How does your pain affect your ability to concentrate, focus, and maintain attention?

[If there are psychological impairments]:

- ◦ Do you ever feel hopeless? Helpless?
- ◦ Have you attempted suicide?
- ◦ Do you have outbursts?
- ◦ Do you avoid people?
- ◦ Do you have panic attacks?
- ◦ Are there days that you stay in bed all day?
- ◦ How has your memory been affected?

## Functional questions

- How much can you life and carry?
- How far or how long can you walk?
  - Do you use a cane?
  - Do you have difficulty with stairs?
  - How long can you stand?
  - How long can you sit?
  - Do you need to shift positions?
  - Is lying down comfortable for you?

- Can you bend at the waist?
- Can you kneel and stoop?
- Can you climb?
- Can you push, reach, and pull?
- What is the most comfortable position for you to be in during the day?

## Personal care questions

- Are you able to bathe yourself?
- Are you able to dress yourself?
- Do you cook your own meals?
- Do you have pets that you care for?
- Do you clean your home?
- Do you go grocery shopping?
- Do you have difficulty sleeping?
- Do you take naps during the day?

## Social questions

- Are you a member of a church or other social organization?
- Do you watch television?
- Do you read?
- What do you read?

- Do you have any hobbies?
- Are there any hobbies that you used to have that you no longer have because of your impairments?
- Do you socialize with family and friends?
- Do you drive?
- Describe a typical day.

*The Vocational Expert*
Once your representative is finished asking you questions, the judge may ask some follow up questions or no questions at all. The judge will then ask the vocational expert to testify.

This is the hard part! I say it's the hard part because you will not be able to respond to these "experts" testifying about your abilities. You will be required to sit at the table and listen to these folks testify without responding. You may not even understand what they are saying because it sounds like they are speaking in a different language, citing numbers and codes. I tell my clients to just zone out at this point. There is nothing you can say or do at this point anyway, it's not worth getting upset over!

If there is a Vocational Expert at your hearing, the Vocational Expert will begin by classifying your past work. You will hear him or her spout out numbers and words like "heavy, medium, light, sedentary" and "skilled or unskilled" and "SVP." It will sound like, well, gobbledygook, for lack of a better term. So what exactly is going on? What are these numbers?

Let me take a few steps back. Before your hearing, the Social Security Administration sent a copy of your work history to the Vocational Expert. This is some of the numerous pages you filled out as part of your application for benefits. If you remember – and you may not because it's been years at this point – you filled out your work history for 15 years prior to when you went out of work. You had to list how much you were required to: sit, stand, lift, carry, etc.

This is what the Vocational Expert has reviewed.

Based on what you wrote, the Vocational Expert will classify your past work as: Sedentary, Light, Medium, or Heavy. I will explain all about these classifications in section VII.

And what exactly are those numbers? The Vocational Expert has been asked to testify according to a large book entitled the "Dictionary of Occupational Titles," or the D.O.T. for short.

Within the D.O.T., every job is classified according to industry, assigned a number code, and given a number to indicate how much training is involved (the SVP) and whether the job is considered "skilled" or "unskilled." The D.O.T. *has not been* updated since 1999. 1999! Relying on data from the 90s when so much has changed technologically is ridiculous! Judges are basing their decisions – in part – on data from the 90s. Unacceptable, in my book! Excuse me while I step down off my soapbox.

Nevertheless, the Social Security Administration has indicated that there will be a new system to replace the D.O.T. in 2019. The new system will be called "Occupational Information System" and my hope is that it will reflect the requirements of the jobs *as they exist today.*

After the Vocational Expert classifies your past work, the Judge will ask the Vocational Expert a series of hypotheticals. At this point, I hope you took my advice and zoned out. If you didn't, your head just might start to spin at this very moment.

These hypotheticals will sound something like this: "Assume an individual with the same past relevant work as this claimant who can lift 10 pounds occasionally, stand and walk 6 hours, sit for 6 out of eight hours, cannot climb ladders or ropes, no crawling, limited to frequent reaching, handling, and fingering; must avoid moving machinery, unprotected heights, limited to simple instructions."

The Judge will then ask the Vocational Expert if the hypothetical individual can perform the claimant's past work and if not, what other jobs could this hypothetical individual perform. At this point, the Vocational Expert may – or may not – list out several jobs, again with their codes and skill ratings.

The Judge will then add another hypothetical and ask the Vocational Expert the same questions – whether this hypothetical individual can perform your past work and if not, what other jobs exist that this person could perform. If you are thinking "this is bananas!" I happen to agree with you, but we must play along with this charade, as it is a required part of the hearing.

After the Judge is finished asking questions, your lawyer (or you, if you are representing yourself) will have a chance to ask the Vocational Expert some questions.

One of my favorite questions to ask is: "Assume an individual who is unable to come to work one day a week. Would that individual be able to perform the claimant's past work? Or any other work?" This exceeds the attendance requirements of all jobs out there, and the Vocational Expert will always answer that there are no jobs that can be performed. Another favorite question of mine has to do with mistakes "after the 30 day learning period, if one mistake is made per day, would that be acceptable?" Again, the Vocational Expert should answer that "this would exceed acceptable workplace tolerances."

Your representative may ask additional questions about the Vocational Expert's testimony, or she or he may not. It is usually a decision that has been carefully considered by your lawyer or representative.

If your lawyer or representative announces to the Judge that she or he will not be asking the Vocational Expert any questions, trust and believe me when I tell you that there's a reason for that. Wait until you are out of the hearing office to ask your lawyer or representative the reason.

*Medical Expert*
If there is a Medical Expert in your case, the Medical Expert will have been sent the medical portion of your file to review. The Medical Expert will testify about your diagnoses and your symptoms and whether your conditions rise to the severity to meet a Listing. (A Listing is an impairment for which the Social Security Administration has set out requirements where, if you meet those requirements, you will be approved for Social Security Disability). Most people have impairments that do not meet a Listing and the inquiry will proceed to your work history.

Again, at this point, if you have a lawyer, your lawyer will handle this part. Your lawyer will get a chance to question the Medical Expert and challenge the Medical Expert's testimony. Again, if your lawyer chooses to ask no questions of the Medical Expert, there's likely a good reason that has been carefully considered.

As a note, each Judge handles hearings differently. I have been in hearings where the Medical Expert testifies first; I have also been in hearings where the Medical Expert testifies last. It depends on who the Judge calls first. Another note: Vocational Experts are very common. Medical Experts are not as common, however, there are some judges that have Medical Experts at every hearing. Again, it all depends on the judge.

After all of the experts testify, the Judge may ask your lawyer to make a closing statement; or, the Judge may not. Your lawyer may or may not choose to make one. I like to make one just so that I have the last word. If your lawyer chooses not to (I will say it again) it was likely the product of much thought and consideration. You may want to ask your lawyer about the choices made in the hearing, but know this: your lawyer is REQUIRED to be your zealous advocate by the State Bar. Your lawyer represents YOU and has prepared for this hearing and thought about every angle.

# After the Hearing

If you are so inclined to ask your lawyer about the decisions made during the hearing, please do so outside of the hearing office. I prefer to discuss details of the hearing outside of the earshot of anyone who works within the hearing office. Call me paranoid, but I know a few people who work in a hearing office (who shall remain nameless) and they have relayed stories to me of what they've heard claimants and their representatives discussing after the hearing. Best to go somewhere else.

The hearing is over! Now what? It should come as no surprise by now that the next step is to wait. How long you wait can vary. Once the hearing is finished, the Judge makes a decision and then hands your case to a decision writer. Decision writers are attorneys that – you guessed it – write the decisions. Once the decision writer is finished, the decision will go to the Judge to review and sign. Unfortunately, there is nothing that you can do to speed up the process.

This process could take two weeks or it could take four months. It all depends on how quickly the Judge made a decision, how quickly the decision writer got the decision out, and how long it took for the Judge to review and sign the decision.

Once you get the decision in the mail, it will be no surprise what the result is because in large, bold letters at the top of the decision, it will announce one of the following: Fully Favorable, Partially Favorable, or Unfavorable.
Fully Favorable means that you won! The Judge agreed with you and the next letter you get will be an award letter explaining all of the

details about exactly how much you will get paid each month and any back pay that you are due.

Partially Favorable means that you won but there's a catch. There are many scenarios as to what the result of a Partially Favorable decision is. Here are two examples: the Judge agreed that you are disabled but decided that you became disabled later than when you alleged (this is called an amended onset, and you will be getting ongoing benefits); the Judge agreed that you are disabled but decided that you were disabled when you went out of work and then improved to the point that you could go back to work (this is called a closed period, meaning that you won't be getting ongoing benefits, rather a lump sum).

An Unfavorable decision means that you lost. If you get an Unfavorable decision, I want you have a moment, but that's it. Just a moment. This is NOT the end. You need to send in an appeal within sixty days.

If you have a lawyer or representative working for you, call that person right away. They will likely want to review the decision. Do not lose hope at this point. You are still disabled, and it's a shame that the judge didn't agree, but this is not the end of the road. Very far from the end, in fact.

# The Appeals Council

Once the Social Security Administration gets your appeal, your file will be sent to the Appeals Council at the Office of Hearing Operations in Falls Church, VA. Your lawyer or representative will be able to send in a brief which details the legal error made in your case and why you are entitled to win. Unfortunately, there is a *long* wait to get a decision back from the Appeals Council – usually around eighteen months.

The Appeals Council can remand your case, which means they will send your case back to the Judge with instructions for the Judge to consider certain evidence or call experts. The Appeals Council can approve your case – you win! Or the Appeals Council can deny your case. after. all. that. waiting.

The Appeals Council isn't required to review every case. In fact, in 2017, the Appeals Council only granted Review to 12.10% of cases that came through. That sounds bleak, but keep in mind that only 30% of cases that could have been appealed (i.e. lost their hearing) actually DID appeal to the Appeals Council in 2017.

If the Appeals Council denies your case, I am pleading with you now, please DO NOT lose hope. At this point, have a discussion with your lawyer or representative, if you have one, about the best course of action. You can file a new application, but depending on the specifics in your case, this may not be the best option.

Should you lose at the Appeals Council. the next step in the process is to file your appeal in Federal District Court. Let's say you lose in Federal District Court, you get to appeal to the Circuit Court of Appeals. If you lose there, you would file for a Writ of Certiorari to the United States Supreme Court. The United States Supreme Court may or may not hear your case. Hopefully, your case will be resolved before you are at this stage.

# PART III

# How SSA Decides
# Disability

# HOW SSA DEFINESDISABILITY

Let's get to the heart of the matter, already. I know you are wondering how the Social Security Administration defines "disability."

"Disability" – as defined by the Social Security Administration – is the inability to engage in any substantial gainful activity by reason of any medically determinable physical or mental impairment which can be expected to result in death or which has lasted or can be expected to last for a continuous period of not less than 12 months, or, if you are 55 and blind inability by reason of such blindness to engage in substantial gainful activity requiring skills or abilities comparable to those of any gainful activity in which the individual has previously engaged with some regularity and over a substantial period of time.

Let me get back to speaking English. What does all of that mean? Let's unpack that definition. The "inability to engage in any substantial gainful activity" means that you are unable to work. There are some exceptions, as we discussed earlier. If you are working and making less than $1,170, you are under what the Social Security Administration considers "substantial gainful activity."

As a side note, cases where claimants are working are very difficult to win because you are put in the awkward position of saying that you can't work when you are actually working. The Social Security Administration will likely say that while you are not earning much money, you are, nevertheless, *able* to work more.

So, unable to work "by reason of any medically determinable physical or mental impairment." A medically determinable impairment is an impairment that results from an anatomical, psysiological, or psychological abnormalities which can be demonstrated by medically acceptable clinical and laboratory diagnostic techniques.

This means that your impairment has to be documented by medically acceptable tests and/or lab results. In other words, if a psychic healer (no offense to psychic healers – they are lovely – but Social Security does not recognize their place in the medical community) diagnoses you with xyzorhombia through his communication with spirits and you are now seeking Social Security Disability benefits for your xyzorhombia, the Social Security Administration will deny your claim because you do not have a medically determinable impairment – i.e. one that shows up on medical testing, either through an exam or on lab tests. In fact, xyzorhombia isn't even recognized (yet) in the medical community as an impairment!

Now we know that you have to be unable to work *because of* an impairment that is documented with clinical or laboratory findings. Your impairment is one that "can be expected to result in death OR which has lasted *or is expected* to last for a continuous 12 months." So, your impairment has to have lasted or is expected to last for a continuous 12 months or it is expected that you will die as a result of your impairments. As mentioned in the definition, there are more lenient rules if you are at least 55 years old and blind.

In summary and very simply, the Social Security Administration defines "disability" as the inability to work because of an impairment that is diagnosable and can be documented in the usual medical ways, by the usual medical people, and has lasted or will last 12 months or result in death.

That's it? Well, of course not! There's more to it than that. To determine whether you meet the definition of disability, the Social Security Administration goes through what they call the "Five Step

Sequential Evaluation Process."

# THE FIVE STEP SEQUENTIAL EVALUATION PROCESS

As you may have guessed, there are five steps to this process. It is a "sequential" process, meaning that if you fail at one of the steps (except for step 3), your Disability claim is denied.

You have to meet the steps in order. There are two ways to get Disability: at Step 3 and at Step 5.  That means that in order to prove that you are disabled, you either have to show that you meet a Listing, at Step 3, or, alternatively, at Step 5, that your Residual Functional Capacity is so deficient that you would be unable to perform the demands of sedentary work; that there is no job that exists that you would be capable of performing. This should all make sense by the time you get to the end!

# Step 1: Substantial Gainful Activity

If you are engaging in Substantial Gainful Activity, you do not move on to the other steps, you are found "not disabled." End of story. Full stop. We have talked a little about the dollar amount of $1,180 (for 2018) and I mentioned that it is difficult to be approved if you are working even if under the dollar amount.

So, what *exactly* is Substantial Gainful Activity?
Substantial Gainful Activity is activity that is both substantial *and* gainful. How's that for a circular answer? Let me explain further.

"Substantial" means doing significant physical or mental activities. "Gainful" means for pay or profit, even if you get no profit from it. That means you can't work in a job and forgo a paycheck just so that earnings don't come up under your record. As a side note, Social Security will consider work without regard to legality. That is, drug dealing is illegal, however, it still may be considered substantial gainful activity because it involves significant physical or mental activities and it is for pay or profit.

As discussed earlier, if you are earning (in 2017) over $1,170 per month, there is a presumption that you are engaging in substantial gainful activity. If you are working, making below $1,170 per month, it is likely that the Social Security Administration will find that your work is substantial and gainful, despite the dollar amount.

# Step 2: Severe Impairment

At Step 2 of the sequential evaluation process, you must have a "severe" impairment. What is a severe impairment? The Social Security Administration defines a "severe" impairment as one that interferes with the ability to perform basic work-related activities.

You must have a medically determinable impairment (as discussed earlier, one that can be demonstrated by clinical and laboratory findings) that has lasted or is expected to last 12 months OR result in death. This is called the duration requirement.

What are "basic work-related activities?" There are two categories of work-related activities: physical and mental. Physical work-related activities are: lifting, carrying, standing, walking, sitting, pushing, and pulling. Mental work-related activities are: the ability to understand, carry out, and remember simple instructions; make simple, work-related judgments and decisions; respond appropriately to supervision, co-workers, and work situations, and deal with changes in a routine work setting.

Therefore, if your impairment – or combination of impairments – interferes with your ability to do any of the activities listed above, you will meet the severity requirement. Step 2 is really a threshold requirement, designed to weed out frivolous claims. Most claimants who have been diagnosed with something that interferes with their ability to work meet Step 2.

## Step 3: Listings of Impairments

At Step 3, the Social Security Administration will find you disabled IF your impairment meets (or equals) one of the Listings of Impairments. The Social Security Administration has designated a list of medical criteria for certain impairments. If you meet the requirements of a Listing, then you will be found disabled with no further questions asked!

There are 14 categories of impairments. Within each category, there are several specific impairments and criteria that you must meet in order to meet that Listing. They can be found at https://www.ssa.gov/disability/professionals/bluebook/AdultListings.htm. I've also listed them in the back of this book at Appendix 1. As an illustration, Listing 1.02 states the following:

**1.02 *Major dysfunction of a joint(s) (due to any cause)***: Characterized by gross anatomical deformity (e.g., subluxation, contracture, bony or fibrous ankylosis, instability) and chronic joint pain and stiffness with signs of limitation of motion or other abnormal motion of the affected joint(s), and findings on appropriate medically acceptable imaging of joint space narrowing, bony destruction, or ankylosis of the affected joint(s). With:

> A. Involvement of one major peripheral weight-bearing joint (i.e., hip, knee, or ankle), resulting in inability to ambulate effectively, as defined in 1.00B2b;
> OR
> B. Involvement of one major peripheral joint in each upper extremity (i.e., shoulder, elbow, or wrist-hand), resulting in inability to perform fine and gross movements effectively, as defined in 1.00B2c.

Therefore, to meet Listing 1.02, your medical records must demonstrate everything that is spelled out in that Listing. Let's say that your medical records don't demonstrate everything that is spelled out in the Listing. Your impairment *may* equal a Listing. The Social Security Administration may analyze your records and come to the conclusion that you don't meet the letter of the law, so to speak, but you do meet the spirit of the law. That is to say that it could be determined that your impairments are limiting to the extent reflected in the Listing. This gives the Social Security Administration some flexibility to find claimants disabled.

Having said that, it is rare that the Social Security Administration will find that an impairment *equals* a Listing. For the most part, a medical expert who testifies at a hearing will testify about whether your impairments equal a Listing and that is usually where I have seen claims granted based on equivalence.

If your impairment meets or equals a Listing, that's it. You win your case! If not, you will move on to Step 4.

*Compassionate Allowances and Terminal Illnesses*
The Compassionate Allowances program expedites review for cases where there are certain impairments identified. Currently, there are 228 impairments that qualify for a compassionate allowance. The same rules are used to evaluate whether someone who is diagnosed with one of these impairments meets the definition of disability. People with an impairment on the compassionate allowance list skip to the front of the line and are approved as quickly as possible. For the most part, these are terminal illnesses that are expected to end in death.

The Compassionate Allowances program was a huge sigh of relief to those of us working in this field because it means that less clients die while waiting for their Social Security Disability benefits.

The entire list of impairments that qualify for the Compassionate Allowances program are listed in Appendix 2.

# Step 4: Past Relevant Work

At Step 4, your Residual Functional Capacity will be determined. Your "Residual Functional Capacity" is what you are physically and mentally able to do with the combination of your impairments. Your Residual Functional Capacity, or RFC, is a determination based on your medical records and the information that you've submitted. If they can't determine your RFC from what your medical records and the other forms that you have filled out, then the Social Security Administration will send you for a Consultative Examination.

Then, the Social Security Administration will classify the exertional level of your past work based on the information that you've provided. Your past work – that is, work that you did in the 15 years prior to becoming disabled – will be classified as: sedentary, light, medium, heavy, or very heavy.

*Sedentary*
Sedentary, according to the Social Security Administration, means: lifting no more than 10 pounds at a time and occasionally lifting or carrying articles like docket files, ledgers, and small tools. Also, the Social Security Administration considers a job to be sedentary if walking and standing are required occasionally and other sedentary criteria are met.

*Light*
Light work, according to the Social Security Administration, involves lifting no more than 20 pounds at a time with frequent lifting or carrying of objects weighing up to 10 pounds. Even though the weight lifted may be very little, a job is in this category when it requires a good deal of walking or standing, or when it involves

sitting most of the time with some pushing and pulling of arm or leg controls.

To be considered capable of performing a full or wide range of light work, you must have the ability to do substantially all of these activities. If someone can do light work, then the Social Security Administration will determine that he or she can also do sedentary work, unless there are additional limiting factors such as loss of fine dexterity or inability to sit for long periods of time.

The major difference between sedentary and light work is that most light jobs -- particularly those at the unskilled level of complexity -- require a person to be standing or walking most of the workday. Another important difference is that the frequent lifting or carrying of objects weighing up to 10 pounds (which is required for the full range of light work) implies that the worker is able to do occasional bending of the stooping type, i.e., for no more than one-third of the workday to bend the body downward and forward by bending the spine at the waist.

*Medium*
Medium work involves lifting no more than 50 pounds at a time with frequent lifting or carrying of objects weighing up to 25 pounds. If someone can do medium work, then the Social Security Administration will determine that he or she can also do sedentary and light work.

*Heavy*
Heavy work involves lifting no more than 100 pounds at a time with frequent lifting or carrying of objects weighing up to 50 pounds. If someone can do heavy work, then the Social Security Administration will determine that he or she can also do medium, light, and sedentary work.

*Very Heavy*

Very heavy work involves lifting objects weighing more than 100 pounds at a time with frequent lifting or carrying of objects weighing 50 pounds or more. If someone can do very heavy work, then the Social Security Administration will determine that he or she can also do heavy, medium, light and sedentary work.

Next, whether your past work was skilled, semi-skilled, or unskilled will be determined. "Skilled," "semi-skilled," and "unskilled" are terms that are used by the Social Security Administration to indicate how long it takes to learn the job.

*Unskilled Work*
Here's how the Social Security Administration defines "unskilled work:" unskilled work is work which needs little or no judgment to do simple duties that can be learned on the job in a short period of time. The job may or may not require considerable strength.

For example, a job is unskilled if the primary work duties are handling, feeding and offbearing (that is, placing or removing materials from machines which are automatic or operated by others), or machine tending, and a person can usually learn to do the job in 30 days, and little specific vocational preparation and judgment are needed. It is important to note that a person does not gain work skills by doing unskilled jobs!

*Semi-Skilled Work*
The Social Security Administration defines "semi-skilled work" as follows: semi-skilled work is work which needs some skills but does not require doing the more complex work duties. Semi-skilled jobs may require alertness and close attention to watching machine processes; or inspecting, testing or otherwise looking for irregularities; or tending or guarding equipment, property, materials, or persons against loss, damage or injury; or other types of activities which are similarly less complex than skilled work, but more complex than unskilled work. A job may be classified as semi-skilled

where coordination and dexterity are necessary, as when hands or feet must be moved quickly to do repetitive tasks.

*Skilled Work*
Skilled work requires qualifications in which a person uses judgment to determine the machine and manual operations to be performed in order to obtain the proper form, quality, or quantity of material to be produced. Skilled work may require laying out work, estimating quality, determining the suitability and needed quantities of materials, making precise measurements, reading blueprints or other specifications, or making necessary computations or mechanical adjustments to control or regulate the work. Other skilled jobs may require dealing with people, facts, or figures or abstract ideas at a high level of complexity.

So, just to recap: your past work had exertional (physical) requirements that were sedentary, light, medium, heavy, or very heavy. Your past work had a skill level associated with it which is mainly based on how long it takes to learn how to do the job.

You're saying "but my job wasn't just physical in nature. It was stressful and I had to deal with the public and it gave me panic attacks, made my hair fall out, and it took 10 years off my life!" (or something like that). The anxiety that you experienced as a result of the stress associated with your past work is called a "non-exertional" limitation.

The Social Security Administration defines a "non-exertional impairment" as one that is medically determinable (i.e., diagnosable) and causes a non-exertional limitation of function or an environmental restriction.

Non-exertional impairments may or may not affect a person's capacity to carry out the primary strength requirements of jobs, and they may or may not significantly narrow the range of work a person can do.

Non-exertional limitations can affect the abilities to reach; to seize, hold, grasp, or turn an object (handle); to bend the legs alone (kneel); to bend the spine alone (stoop) or bend both the spine and legs (crouch). Fine movements of small objects, such as done in much sedentary work and in certain types of more demanding work (e.g., surgery), require use of the fingers to pick, pinch, etc. Impairments of vision, speech, and hearing are non-exertional.

Psychological impairments are generally considered non-exertional, but depression and conversion disorders may limit exertion. Although some impairments may cause both exertional limitations and environmental restriction (e.g., a respiratory impairment may limit a person to light work exertion as well as prohibit exposure to excessive dust or fumes), other impairments may result in only environmental restrictions (e.g., skin allergies may only prohibit contact with certain liquids).

Your exertional and non-exertional limitations will be considered when determining your residual functional capacity. Similarly, the non-exertional aspects of your past work will be determined.

Once your residual functional capacity is determined and your past work classified, the question becomes "can you – with your residual functional capacity – return to your past work?" That is, with your current exertional and non-exertional limitations, can you return to any job that you've held in the 15 years prior to when you went out of work?

If the answer is "no," then you move on to Step 5. If the answer is "yes," then you will be found "not disabled."

As a side note, if the Social Security Administration finds that you are able to return to your past relevant work, then there will likely be testimony from a Vocational Expert at your hearing and your attorney (or representative) will have a chance to cross examine the Vocational Expert. If, at your hearing, there was no Vocational Expert and the Judge found that you were able to return to your past work, please see an attorney (if you don't have one) immediately because this is a great issue for appeal.

# Step 5: Other Work

You get to Step 5 after a finding that, with your Residual Functional Capacity, you are unable to return to any of your past relevant work. "Past relevant work" is work that you performed 15 years prior to going out of work due to your impairments.

At Step 5, the question is "is there any other work that exists in the regional or national economy in significant numbers that you can perform with your Residual Functional Capacity, considering your age, education, and past work experience?" Let's take this apart. Many of my clients think this step is unfair, especially if they had highly skilled work. Some comments from my clients: "How can they expect me to work as a greeter? I have a PhD in microbiology!" "How can they tell me that I can be a mattress tester? I've never even heard of that job!"

Here's the deal: the jobs only have to exist in significant numbers in the national economy. That means that there has to be more than 135 jobs regionally and 1,680 nationally. Where did those numbers come from, you might ask? Here's the thing: no one has defined a specific number that constitutes "significant numbers," however, the Ninth Circuit, in a case called Beltran v. Astrue (2012), decided that 135 jobs in the regional economy and 1,680 jobs in the national economy did not qualify as "significant numbers." So, there needs to be *more* than 135 regionally and 1,680 nationally for the Social Security Administration to claim that a specific job exists in "significant numbers."

The other work that exists in significant numbers has to be compatible with your residual functional capacity (remember, that's the maximum that you can do with your impairments). When considering whether there is other work that you can do, the Social Security Administration will consider your age, education, and past work experience.

*Medical-Vocational Guidelines or Grid Rules*
The Social Security Administration has provided guidelines to determine whether someone is disabled. These guidelines are formally called the "Medical-Vocational Guidelines" and often referred to as the "grids" or the "grid rules." The grid rules are officially found at Appendix 2 to Subpart P of Part 404, but that's not something that you need to know.

Those rules will provide a determination based on a combination of factors: age, education, and whether past work was skilled, semi-skilled, or unskilled. The grid rules were developed in an attempt to standardize decisions across the country. The older someone is, the easier it is to be found disabled based on these rules, as you will see.

*Age*
The Social Security Administration has broken up age categories as follows: a "younger individual" is someone between the ages of 18 and 49 years old; an "individual approaching advanced age" is someone between the ages of 50 and 54; and "individual of advanced age" is someone over 55 years old.

*Education*
The Social Security Administration has categories of education, as well: high school or more, limited or less, or illiterate or unable to communicate in English. "High school or more" is self-explanatory. You may have never heard of "limited or less," though. A "limited" education means a 7th grade through the 11th grade level of formal education. "Less" than a limited education would be a "marginal" education, which means 6th grade or less. Finally, "illiterate" is the

inability to read and the inability to communicate in English is in that group.

*Transferrable Skills*
The grid rules mention transferrable skills, in some cases. Here's what they mean by transferrable skills: skills that were learned in your past work that can be used in another job. You can only get transferrable skills from semi-skilled or skilled jobs, by the way. If your past work was unskilled, you have no transferrable skills (no offense).

So, how do they figure out of I have transferrable skills? Luckily, they aren't going to put you through any sort of job test. The Social Security Administration says that it is likely that you have transferrable skills to a new job if the new job involves the same skills (or less), same or similar tools and machines are used, and the same or similar raw materials, products, processes or services are involved. Then they say that if the skills you obtained from your past work are so specialized (like mining, agriculture, or fishing) or acquired in an isolated setting and you can't use those skills in another setting, then you will have no transferrable skills.

If you are over 55, the Social Security Administration has given you a little gift and says that if you are limited to sedentary exertional level, there must be very little, if any vocational adjustment required in terms of tools, work processes, work settings or the industry. The same is true for individuals who are age 60 and older and are limited to light work exertion. What does that mean? The new job has to be almost identical to your old job.

*Direct Entry into Skilled Work*
Another term you will see on the grid rules that is confusing and you've probably never heard before is "provides" or "does not provide for direct entry into skilled work." This just means that you've recently completed education that would qualify you for a different

skilled job. So, "does not provide for direct entry into unskilled work" means that you haven't completed any new education that would allow you to get a new, skilled job.

The great thing about the grid rules is that you can be physically capable of performing a level of work and still found disabled! For example, someone who is limited to the sedentary exertional level, is of "advanced age," has a high school education, and past work is unskilled will be found disabled under the grid rules.

The grid rules are sometimes used as a *framework* for decision-making. That just means that where, let's say, someone's residual functional capacity falls between two categories, like light and sedentary, or where there are non-exertional limitations, which involve mental impairments or manipulative limitations, then the grid rules will be used as a suggestion. If the grid rules say that you are disabled, then you should be found disabled.

*How to use the Medical Vocational Guidelines or Grid Rules*
Below, I have the actual tables used by the Social Security Administration. To use these lovely rules, you need to know your residual functional capacity: sedentary, light, or medium. Go to the table that uses your particular level. Once you find the correct table, then you would go to your age category (younger individual, closely approaching advanced age, advanced age).

Then, find your education level. If you have recently completed education, you would choose "provides for direct entry into skilled work." If you haven't then, you would choose "does not provide for direct entry into skilled work."

Then, find the skill level of your past work. The last box will be either "disabled" or "not disabled." If you got disabled, then congratulations! It's almost like playing BINGO! If your box says "not disabled," don't lose hope! There is yet another way to show that you are disabled, so stick with me and keep reading.

Table 1 – Limited to Sedentary

| Rule | Age | Education | Previous work experience | Decision |
|------|-----|-----------|--------------------------|----------|
| 201.01 | Advanced age | Limited or less | Unskilled or none | Disabled |
| 201.02 | Advanced age | Limited or less | Skilled or semiskilled— skills not transferable | Disabled |
| 201.03 | Advanced age | Limited or less | Skilled or semiskilled— skills transferable | Not disabled |
| 201.04 | Advanced age | High school graduate or more—does not provide for direct entry into skilled work | Unskilled or none | Disabled |
| 201.05 | Advanced age | High school graduate or more—provides for direct entry into skilled work | Unskilled or none | Not disabled |
| 201.06 | Advanced age | High school graduate or more—does not provide for direct entry into skilled work | Skilled or semiskilled— skills not transferable | Disabled |
| 201.07 | Advanced age | High school graduate or more—does not provide for direct entry into skilled work | Skilled or semiskilled— skills transferable | Not disabled |

| Rule | Age | Education | Previous work experience | Decision |
|---|---|---|---|---|
| 201.08 | Advanced age | High school graduate or more—provides for direct entry into skilled work | Skilled or semiskilled—skills not transferable | Not disabled |
| 201.09 | Closely approaching advanced age | Limited or less | Unskilled or none | Disabled |
| 201.10 | Closely approaching advanced age | Limited or less | Skilled or semiskilled—skills not transferable | Disabled |
| 201.11 | Closely approaching advanced age | Limited or less | Skilled or semiskilled—skills transferable | Not disabled |
| 201.12 | Closely approaching advanced age | High school graduate or more—does not provide for direct entry into skilled work | Unskilled or none | Disabled |
| 201.13 | Closely approaching advanced age | High school graduate or more—provides for direct entry into skilled work | Unskilled or none | Not disabled |
| 201.14 | Closely approaching advanced age | High school graduate or more—does not provide for direct entry into skilled work | Skilled or semiskilled—skills not transferable | Disabled |

| Rule | Age | Education | Previous work experience | Decision |
|------|-----|-----------|--------------------------|----------|
| 201.15 | Closely approaching advanced age | High school graduate or more—does not provide for direct entry into skilled work | Skilled or semiskilled—skills transferable | Not disabled |
| 201.16 | Closely approaching advanced age | High school graduate or more—provides for direct entry into skilled work | Skilled or semiskilled—skills not transferable | Not disabled |
| 201.17 | Younger individual age 45-49 | Illiterate or unable to communicate in English | Unskilled or none | Disabled |
| 201.18 | Younger individual age 45-49 | Limited or less—at least literate and able to communicate in English | Unskilled or none | Not disabled |
| 201.19 | Younger individual age 45-49 | Limited or less | Skilled or semiskilled—skills not transferable | Not disabled |
| 201.20 | Younger individual age 45-49 | Limited or less | Skilled or semiskilled—skills transferable | Not disabled |
| 201.21 | Younger individual age 45-49 | High school graduate or more | Skilled or semiskilled—skills not transferable | Not disabled |

| Rule | Age | Education | Previous work experience | Decision |
|---|---|---|---|---|
| 201.22 | Younger individual age 45-49 | High school graduate or more | Skilled or semiskilled—skills transferable | Not disabled |
| 201.23 | Younger individual age 18-44 | Illiterate or unable to communicate in English | Unskilled or none | Not disabled |
| 201.24 | Younger individual age 18-44 | Limited or less—at least literate and able to communicate in English | Unskilled or none | Not disabled |
| 201.25 | Younger individual age 18-44 | Limited or less | Skilled or semiskilled—skills not transferable | Not disabled |
| 201.26 | Younger individual age 18-44 | Limited or less | Skilled or semiskilled—skills transferable | Not disabled |
| 201.27 | Younger individual age 18-44 | High school graduate or more | Unskilled or none | Not disabled |
| 201.28 | Younger individual age 18-44 | High school graduate or more | Skilled or semiskilled—skills not transferable | Not disabled |
| 201.29 | Younger individual age 18-44 | High school graduate or more | Skilled or semiskilled—skills transferable | Not disabled |

Table 2 – Limited to Light

| Rule | Age | Education | Previous work experience | Decision |
|---|---|---|---|---|
| 202.01 | Advanced age | Limited or less | Unskilled or none | Disabled |
| 202.02 | Advanced age | Limited or less | Skilled or semiskilled—skills not transferable | Disabled |
| 202.03 | Advanced age | Limited or less | Skilled or semiskilled—skills transferable | Not disabled |
| 202.04 | Advanced age | High school graduate or more—does not provide for direct entry into skilled work | Unskilled or none | Disabled |
| 202.05 | Advanced age | High school graduate or more—provides for direct entry into skilled work | Unskilled or none | Not disabled |
| 202.06 | Advanced age | High school graduate or more—does not provide for direct entry into skilled work | Skilled or semiskilled—skills not transferable | Disabled |
| 202.07 | Advanced age | High school graduate or more—does not provide for direct entry into skilled work | Skilled or semiskilled—skills transferable | Not disabled |

| Rule | Age | Education | Previous work experience | Decision |
|---|---|---|---|---|
| 202.08 | Advanced age | High school graduate or more—provides for direct entry into skilled work | Skilled or semiskilled—skills not transferable | Not disabled |
| 202.09 | Closely approaching advanced age | Illiterate or unable to communicate in English | Unskilled or none | Disabled |
| 202.10 | Closely approaching advanced age | Limited or less – at least literate and able to communicate in English | Unskilled or none | Not disabled |
| 202.11 | Closely approaching advanced age | Limited or less | Skilled or semiskilled—skills not transferable | Not disabled |
| 202.12 | Closely approaching advanced age | Limited or less | Skilled or semiskilled—skills transferable | Not disabled |
| 202.13 | Closely approaching advanced age | High school graduate or more | Unskilled or none | Not disabled |
| 202.14 | Closely approaching advanced age | High school graduate or more | Skilled or semiskilled—skills not transferable | Not disabled |

| Rule | Age | Education | Previous work experience | Decision |
|---|---|---|---|---|
| 202.15 | Closely approaching advanced age | High school graduate or more | Skilled or semiskilled—skills transferable | Not disabled |
| 202.16 | Younger individual | Illiterate or unable to communicate in English | Unskilled or none | Not disabled |
| 202.17 | Younger individual | Limited or less – at least literate and able to communicate in English | Unskilled or none | Not disabled |
| 202.18 | Younger individual | Limited or less | Skilled or semiskilled—skills not transferable | Not disabled |
| 202.19 | Younger individual | Limited or less | Skilled or semiskilled—skills transferable | Not disabled |
| 202.20 | Younger individual | High school graduate or more | Unskilled or none | Not disabled |
| 202.21 | Younger individual | High school graduate or more | Skilled or semiskilled—skills not transferable | Not disabled |
| 202.22 | Younger individual | High school graduate or more | Skilled or semiskilled—skills transferable | Not disabled |

Table 3 – Limited to Medium

| Rule | Age | Education | Previous work experience | Decision |
|------|-----|-----------|--------------------------|----------|
| 203.01 | Closely approaching retirement age | Marginal or none | Unskilled or none | Disabled. |
| 203.02 | Closely approaching retirement age | Limited or less | None | Disabled |
| 203.03 | Closely approaching retirement age | Limited | Unskilled | Not disabled |
| 203.04 | Closely approaching retirement age | Limited or less | Skilled or semiskilled—skills not transferable | Not disabled |
| 203.05 | Closely approaching retirement age | Limited or less | Skilled or semiskilled—skills transferable | Not disabled |
| 203.06 | Closely approaching retirement age | High school graduate or more | Unskilled or none | Not disabled |
| 203.07 | Closely approaching retirement age | High school graduate or more—does not provide for direct entry into skilled work | Skilled or semiskilled—skills not transferable | Not disabled |

| Rule | Age | Education | Previous work experience | Decision |
|---|---|---|---|---|
| 203.08 | Closely approaching retirement age | High school graduate or more—does not provide for direct entry into skilled work | Skilled or semiskilled—skills transferable | Not disabled |
| 203.09 | Closely approaching retirement age | High school graduate or more—provides for direct entry into skilled work | Skilled or semiskilled—skills not transferable | Not disabled |
| 203.10 | Advanced age | Limited or less | None | Disabled |
| 203.11 | Advanced age | Limited or less | Unskilled | Not disabled |
| 203.12 | Advanced age | Limited or less | Skilled or semiskilled—skills not transferable | Not disabled |
| 203.13 | Advanced age | Limited or less | Skilled or semiskilled—skills transferable | Not disabled |
| 203.14 | Advanced age | High school graduate or more | Unskilled or none | Not disabled |
| 203.15 | Advanced age | High school graduate or more—does not provide for direct entry into skilled work | Skilled or semiskilled—skills not transferable | Not disabled |
| 203.16 | Advanced age | High school graduate or more—does not provide for direct entry into skilled work | Skilled or semiskilled—skills transferable | Not disabled |

| Rule | Age | Education | Previous work experience | Decision |
|------|-----|-----------|--------------------------|----------|
| 203.17 | Advanced age | High school graduate or more—provides for direct entry into skilled work | Skilled or semiskilled—skills not transferable | Not disabled |
| 203.18 | Closely approaching advanced age | Limited or less | Unskilled or none | Not disabled |
| 203.19 | Closely approaching advanced age | Limited or less | Skilled or semiskilled—skills not transferable | Not disabled |
| 203.20 | Closely approaching advanced age | Limited or less | Skilled or semiskilled—skills transferable | Not disabled |
| 203.21 | Closely approaching advanced age | High school graduate or more | Unskilled or none | Not disabled |
| 203.22 | Closely approaching advanced age | High school graduate or more—does not provide for direct entry into skilled work | Skilled or semiskilled—skills not transferable | Not disabled |
| 203.23 | Closely approaching advanced age | High school graduate or more—does not provide for direct entry into skilled work | Skilled or semiskilled—skills transferable | Not disabled |

| Rule | Age | Education | Previous work experience | Decision |
|---|---|---|---|---|
| 203.24 | Closely approaching advanced age | High school graduate or more—provides for direct entry into skilled work | Skilled or semiskilled—skills not transferable | Not disabled |
| 203.25 | Younger individual | Limited or less | Unskilled or none | Not disabled |
| 203.26 | Younger individual | Limited or less | Skilled or semiskilled—skills not transferable | Not disabled |
| 203.27 | Younger individual | Limited or less | Skilled or semiskilled—skills transferable | Not disabled |
| 203.28 | Younger individual | High school graduate or more | Unskilled or none | Not disabled |
| 203.29 | Younger individual | High school graduate or more—does not provide for direct entry into skilled work | Skilled or semiskilled—skills not transferable | Not disabled |
| 203.30 | Younger individual | High school graduate or more—does not provide for direct entry into skilled work | Skilled or semiskilled—skills transferable | Not disabled |
| 203.31 | Younger individual | High school graduate or more—provides for direct entry into skilled work | Skilled or semiskilled—skills not transferable | Not disabled |

*Less than Sedentary*

Let's say that the grid rules would find you "not disabled." Recall from before that I said that these rules are only used as a framework, or as a suggestion, if you also have non-exertional limitations or impairments. That means that perhaps physically, you can do sedentary work, but you also suffer from depression. Depression is an impairment that affects your ability to concentrate and focus – these are non-exertional limitations. So then, the grid rules are only used as a suggestion.

Ok, so now you are thoroughly confused by the grid rules and besides, you can't even do what they call sedentary activity! What now? Well, it is possible that your residual functional capacity – remember, that's the maximum that you can do now with your impairments, restrictions, and limitations – is *less* than sedentary.

A residual functional capacity of less than sedentary means that you are able to lift less than 10 pounds and you are unable to sit for most of an 8-hour day. Since sedentary is the least exertional of all of the exertional levels, a residual functional capacity of less than sedentary means that there are no jobs that you would be able to perform. If you are a younger individual with only a physical impairment or the grid rules would find you "not disabled," then less than sedentary is exactly where you need to be at this stage in the game. Otherwise, you will be found "not disabled."

# Other Issues

**Disability from other agencies like Veteran's Administration and NFL**

So, you have been found disabled by the V.A. (or NFL or some similar agency). You are thinking you should be a shoe-in for Social Security Disability, am I right? You would be oh-so-wrong.

The Social Security Administration will consider evidence from other disability programs, but they will not automatically find you disabled because another program did.

If you've been found 100% permanent and total by the V.A., then the good news is that the Social Security Administration will expedite your case (see section entitled 'Cases that Can be Expedited'), to the extent they can. What does that mean? Well, if it takes them a while to get your records, or if you have to go for a Consultative Examination, then you are probably looking at the same timeline as everyone else.

If you've only been found partially disabled by the V.A. and not 100%, then you are on the same track as everyone else, unfortunately. Anything less than 100% doesn't get expedited.

In the end, they will not just 'go with' someone else's determination that you are disabled, but they will look at the evidence used to make the determination that you are disabled and see if it meets the Social Security Administration's definition of disability.

Most of the time, if you have been found disabled by another program, there was a lot of evidence generated and used to support your disability claim. Lots of tests have been done and your doctors have most likely written numerous letters supporting your claim. That's all good for your Social Security Disability claim and it will all be considered in deciding whether you meet Social Security's definition of disability.

**Worker's Compensation**
You got injured on the job. You've likely been to more examinations that you can count. You may have had a hearing or been to a settlement conference. There was probably a lawyer representing your employer fighting against your claim. You probably have thought or said something along the lines of "this is the thanks I get for busting my you-know-what for all those years?!"

The good news is that you probably have lots of medical records! That is very good for your Social Security Disability case. The bad news is that Social Security will offset for Worker's Compensation benefits. It's a complicated formula, but I am going to try and explain it!

*How does SSA offset work for Worker's Compensation benefits?*
Let's say you received a lump sum. To calculate how much the Social Security Administration would offset, the Social Security Administration first calculates what your maximum amount of benefits would be – they call this the "applicable limit." The applicable limit is 80% of your pre-injury income, which is what the Social Security Administration calls your "average current earnings." They calculate your average current earnings by taking the highest of: (1) the average monthly wage that your Social Security Disability benefit amount is based on (SSA calls this your unindexed PIA); (2) the average monthly earnings from the highest 5 years in a row (high 5); (3) the average monthly earnings from a single calendar year (high 1).

Then, to determine your applicable limit, the Social Security Administration will take 80% of your average current earnings. the Social Security Administration will then add your monthly Social Security Disability payment to your monthly worker's compensation payment. the Social Security Administration will reduce your payments until it the applicable limit is reached. Because you got a lump sum, the Social Security Administration will look at the worker's compensation settlement agreement to calculate your monthly amount and reduce it based on that amount.

So, as an example, you got a lump sum of $12,000. This averages $1,000 per month. Your pre-injury average earnings were $2,000 per month. You are found disabled by the Social Security Administration and entitled to ongoing benefits. You are entitled to $1,500 per month from the Social Security Administration. Then the Social Security Administration comes along and says "not so fast!" They will reduce your total monthly payment so that it meets 80% of $2,000. So, figuring $1,000 from worker's comp, the Social Security Administration will pay you $600 to bring you up to $1,600 which is 80% of $2,000.

## Drug and Alcohol Addiction

Before 1996, if you had a drug or alcohol addiction, then you could get Social Security Disability because of your addiction. Addiction was your disability! This is an interesting fact that may earn you some points at trivia, but nothing that you need to know for your case.

The current law is the "Senior Citizen's Right to Work Act of 1996" that eliminated Drug and Alcohol Addiction as a basis for Disability. The Act says that individuals are not disabled if the drug and alcohol addiction is a contributing factor to the individual's disability.

That is to say that if your disability would exist in the absence of drug and alcohol abuse, then you can properly be found disabled. If, on the other hand, your drug and alcohol addiction contributes to your disability, then the Social Security Administration will find you not disabled.

If there is evidence in your file of a drug or alcohol problem, then the Social Security Administration has to determine whether your disability would stand alone or whether your drug and alcohol addiction adds to your disability. This is an especially difficult task when there are psychological impairments involved.

To figure out how your drug and alcohol addiction has or has not contributed to your disability, the Social Security Administration will look at periods of abstinence and compare the physical and psychological findings during that time and during a period when you were using. If there is no point of abstinence, get a statement from a treating physician explaining how your drug and alcohol addiction does not contribute to your disability.

**Medical Records**
Medical records are essential to proving your Social Security Disability claim. Let me say that again: medical records are essential to proving your Social Security Disability claim. You cannot win your case if you do not have medical records to back up your claims.

Let's say you can't afford to see a doctor. You must make every effort humanly possible to see a doctor! Without medical records, you have no case and without a case, you will get no benefits. Borrow the money, investigate whether there are free clinics …. Anything you can. You must have medical records!

Not only are medical records essential, but they have to back up your complaints. Why do I mention this? Well, lots of times, I have clients that tell me absolutely horrific stories of how they are barely surviving from day to day. The pain is so bad they can't get out of bed most days. They are unable to dress themselves and they rely on others to cook meals and drive. They tell me these things, and then I look at their medical records from their treating physicians and it says nothing even close to anything that they have told me. In fact, I've seen medical records that say "patient doing well" and "no complaints from patient." These kinds of notations in your medical records can kill your Social Security case!

The records from your doctor MUST accurately reflect your complaints. That's nice, you say, but you have no idea what your doctor is writing! Here's what I suggest to prevent this from happening: (preferably before you apply, but if you've already applied, it is ok) have a conversation with your doctor letting your doctor know that you are applying for Social Security Disability. Let your doctor know why you think you can't work. Tell your doctor that you would appreciate it if your complaints are accurately reflected in her notes. Then, after each visit, request your medical records. If you see something that is incorrect or that does not accurately reflect what you have told your doctor, then, by all means, ask your doctor to correct it. Most of the time, doctors want to help their patients and are very receptive to these requests.

The next thing that you need to be aware of is the type of medical professional you are getting treatment from. You MUST have documentation from medical sources who have performed diagnostic testing and who have documented clinical findings. BUT not all of your medical sources are considered "acceptable medical sources!" While Social Security will look at all of your medical records, they will give less weight to non-acceptable medical sources.

*Acceptable Medical Sources*
An "acceptable medical source" is a medical source that the Social Security Administration has determined is "Acceptable." How is that for a circular answer?

To figure this out, the Social Security Administration has a list! The following are considered "acceptable medical sources:"
- Licensed physicians (M.D. or O.D.).

- Licensed or certified psychologists at the independent practice level.

- School psychologists, or other licensed or certified individuals with other titles who perform the same function as a school psychologist in a school setting, are AMSs for impairments of intellectual disability, learning disabilities, and borderline intellectual functioning only.

- Licensed optometrists for impairments of visual disorders, or measurement of visual acuity and visual fields only, depending on the scope of practice in the State in which the optometrist practices.

- Licensed podiatrists for impairments of the foot, or foot and ankle only, depending on whether the State in which the podiatrist practices permits the practice of podiatry on the foot only, or the foot and ankle.

- Qualified speech-language pathologists (SLPs) for speech or language impairments only. For this source, "qualified" means that the SLP must be licensed by the State professional licensing agency, or be fully certified by the State education agency in the State that he or she practices, or hold a Certificate of Clinical Competence in Speech-Language-Pathology from the American Speech-Language Hearing Association.

- For cases filed on or after March 27, 2017, licensed physician assistants for impairments within the licensed scope of practice only.
- For cases filed on or after March 27, 2017, licensed audiologists for impairments of hearing loss, auditory processing disorders, and balance disorders within the licensed scope of practice only.
- For cases filed on or after March 27, 2017, licensed Advanced Practice Registered Nurses (APRN), also known in some States as Advanced Practice Nurse (APN), and Advanced Registered Nurse Practitioner (ARNP) for impairments within his or her licensed scope of practice.

There are four types of APRNs with a handful of State variations:
1. Certified Nurse Midwife (CNM);
2. Nurse Practitioner (NP);
3. Certified Registered Nurse Anesthetist (CRNA); and
4. Clinical Nurse Specialist (CNS).

That's a long list, but it's important to note who is NOT on the list: Marriage Family Therapists (or other therapists), Licensed Social Workers, Chiropractors, Naturopaths, and Registered Nurses.

You may notice that for cases that were filed after March 27, 2017, there is a longer list. That's because the law changed then. Now, there are many more "Acceptable Medical Sources," but there is still room for improvement!

So, if your primary source of treatment is from a chiropractor for your back problem, for example, and you submit the medical records from your chiropractor to support your disability claim, make sure that you are also seeing a physician (an M.D. or D.O.). It's the same if your only evidence of your mental impairment is from a counselor or LCSW, for example. Make sure that you are also seeing a psychiatrist or psychologist.

And while the Social Security Administration has to consider all of your records, they are more likely to deny you if you only have evidence from medical sources that are deemed "not acceptable." They will take the Consultative Examination Doctor's word over your non-acceptable medical source to deny your claim.

It doesn't matter that you have finally found a treatment provider that: believes you, is supportive of your disability claim, has written letters on your behalf IF that treatment provider is not an acceptable medical source. It's a huge bummer, to say the least, when great evidence isn't given full weight simply because of the lack of initials behind someone's name.

Make sure that you are seeing an acceptable medical source so this doesn't happen to you!

*How to Get your Records*
Getting your records is probably easier than you think. Your doctor is required by law to release your records to you at no cost. Your doctor can charge anyone else who requests your records (with your permission). In fact, I've seen some doctors charge $25 per page! That is why many Representatives ask you to get your records and forward them to your Representative. It's a cost-saving measure. Because your Representative can charge you for things like medical records, it is to your benefit to try and get your records for free!

It is your responsibility to get your records, so make sure that you are on top of this. I give my clients a fax number and tell them to request that their records are faxed to my fax line after every few visits.

## Statements from Doctors

Statements from treating doctors are an excellent way to prove that you are disabled. These statements can go a long way, provided that your doctor's statement is consistent with his or her medical records.

For example, if your doctor fills out a form saying that you are unable to walk for more than 30 minutes but all of your medical records from that particular doctor say that you have no difficulty walking or standing, then the Social Security Administration will likely say that your doctor's statement that you are unable to walk for more than 30 minutes is inconsistent with his or her own medical records and it will be given less weight. In other words, they won't pay attention to it!

So, if you give your doctor a statement to fill out, make sure that it is in line with his or her medical records!

What if your doctor refuses to fill out a statement? Well, you can't make anyone do anything. You don't absolutely need a statement from your doctor, but if your doctor refuses, I would figure out what the reason is that your doctor is refusing. Some doctors just don't fill out statements or forms at all. If that's the case, then just move on. If, however, your doctor is refusing to fill out a statement because he or she does not think that you are disabled, then I suggest finding out why your doctor thinks this is the case. Many doctors don't understand the process or what Social Security considers to be the definition of disability. However, if your doctor has some serious reservations about whether what you are reporting as far as your symptoms are true, then, again, I would just move on.

If your doctor fills out a statement that IS unfavorable, then you (and/or your representative) are still required to submit it to Social Security! That means that the judge or, if you have not yet requested a hearing, then the adjudicator at DDS who is evaluating your case will use that statement to deny your case. You don't want to be in that situation! So, if you get any pushback from your doctor about filling out a statement or a form, just move on because no statement is better than a bad one!

In Appendix 3, I have provided sample forms to give your doctors to fill out. These are general forms, but they request the essential information regarding your Residual Functional Capacity. There is one for physical impairments and one for psychological impairments. You can also go to my website at www.helpwithdisability.net and download these forms.


**5 Day Rule**
Back in the day, you could go to your hearing without all of the medical records in your file. Most judges would routinely "leave the record open" and give you a certain number of days to get the missing evidence in. This led to a lot of cases being "open" and it became a hassle for the judges' staff to keep track of all of the missing evidence. Moreover, judges weren't closing cases which led to longer delays.

In 2017, the Social Security Administration implemented a "5 Day Rule." This rule requires Social Security applicants to submit all evidence 5 days prior to their hearing. If, for some reason, you can't get all of the evidence in, the law requires you to "inform" the judge that you are missing evidence. This can be done simply with a letter stating that you have attempted to get the records (include the dates) and that, as of the date of the letter, you have been unable to obtain the records. If you have made a reasonable effort to get the records, the judge will keep the record open (usually 14 to 30 days) for you to obtain and submit the records.

What happens if you submit evidence before the hearing but less than 5 days before the hearing or even at the hearing? In that case, you need "good cause."

You have "good cause" when you can show:
(1) Social Security's action misled you;
(2) You had a physical, mental, educational, or linguistic limitation(s) that prevented you from submitting the evidence earlier; or
(3) Some other unusual, unexpected, or unavoidable circumstance beyond your control prevented you from submitting the evidence earlier.

If you didn't submit a letter informing the judge that you have outstanding medical records (or other records), then you can submit the records with a letter describing your "good cause." The judge may or may not find that you have good cause; this decision depends on the judge.

What happens if you find out about records after the hearing? In that case, you need good cause AND you must show that there is a reasonable possibility that the evidence (alone or when considered with the other evidence of record) would affect the outcome of your case.

Word to the wise: get your medical records (and other records) in before the 5 day deadline!

## Who can Represent Me?
You can represent yourself! You can gather all of your medical records, submit them, prepare for your hearing, and even make arguments on your own behalf. Here's what I know about you, though: you are disabled! You stopped working because of a physical and or mental impairment that prevents you from doing basic work activities.

Representing yourself is a lot like work. In fact, people like me represent people like you on a full-time basis. If you choose to represent yourself, you have started out doing the right thing by reading this book. I still recommend that you find someone to represent you. If you are suspicious of lawyers (I get it – my own father is suspicious of lawyers!), then you have the option of getting a non-attorney representative to represent you.

A "non-attorney representative" is someone who is not an attorney (thank you, Captain Obvious!) but has been approved by the Social Security Administration to represent people seeking Social Security Disability benefits. These people have to be 'of good character' and, if they want to be paid directly by Social Security for their services, then they have to pass a test about Social Security law and carry liability insurance. Non-attorney representatives, for the most part, represent Social Security applicants exclusively. I recommend going to the National Association of Disability Representatives' (NADR) website to find a referral in your area: www.nadr.org. NADR is a wonderful organization that provides continuing education and resources for representatives.

If you are ok with attorneys, you can hire an attorney (like myself) to represent you. Attorneys have to be licensed in at least one state to represent clients across the country in Social Security cases. This is different than, say, a criminal case where you need a lawyer to be a member of the bar in your particular state. Social Security is a federal program and the Social Security Administration decides who can practice before it. I have represented clients in almost every state in Social Security Disability hearings, and I know that many of my colleagues do as well. You can easily find an attorney in your area by visiting the website for the National Organization for Social Security Claimants' Representatives (NOSSCR) at www.nosscr.org. They will only pass along the name of an attorney in your area if they have professional liability insurance and if they are accepting referrals. NOSSCR is another wonderful organization that provides yearly conferences with continuing education, lobbying efforts in the interest of Social Security applicants, support, and resources for representatives.

The benefits of hiring either a non-attorney or an attorney to represent you: your representative or attorney is very familiar with the Social Security rules and regulations. Your representative or attorney will have access to an online system called "Electronic Records Express" after you request a hearing. That way, your representative or attorney can submit all of your medical records electronically. (Regular people don't have access to this system).

Your representative or attorney can submit legal arguments on your behalf and can evaluate the strength of your case. Your representative or attorney will take the stress off of you; going through this process alone can be anxiety-inducing and overwhelming! Your representative or attorney will prepare you for your hearing and give you the confidence you need. Your representative or attorney will cross-examine the experts (either Vocational Expert or Medical Expert) at your hearing.

Here are some questions that you may ask a potential non-attorney or attorney representative:

- How many clients do you have?
- Will I mostly be communicating with you or your staff?
- How long have you been practicing?
- Do you exclusively practice Social Security Disability?
- Are you a member or NADR or NOSSCR?
- Do you have professional liability insurance?

*How much can my representative charge?*
The Social Security Administration sets the amounts that attorneys and non-attorneys alike can charge. Currently, you can only be charged 25% of your backpay, up to $6,000, whichever is less. Your representative may have to pay to get your medical records and can pass on those charges. You should be charged nothing up front and

the fee agreement between you and your representative must be in writing. The fee agreement between you and your representative must be approved by the Social Security Administration.

Most representatives use a standard fee agreement, so that it will be easily approved by the Social Security Administration. The nice thing for both you and your representative is that the fee is withheld from your backpay. That means that you don't have to write a check to your representative when everything is said and done. That also means that if you lose, you owe your representative nothing. Of course, your representative *can* pass on the charges for your medical records and your representative may bill you. Most representatives that I know understand that most people applying for Social Security Disability are in tight financial situations and unable to afford the costs to get their medical records. Because of that, most representatives won't send you a bill for medical records when they know that you are struggling to pay for food.

**Work Attempts**
If you try and go back to work, will it kill your Social Security Disability case? It depends!
If you are struggling to make ends meet and think there's a possibility that you could potentially go back to work, you are allowed to try it out, but it can hurt your case if your work attempt lasts longer than 6 months. If you can't meet the requirements of your job due to your disability and have to stop working before 6 months is up, this is what is called an "unsuccessful work attempt." I actually like it when my clients have unsuccessful work attempts because it is actual evidence that you can't meet the requirements of a job. It is not speculation – you tried and have proof that you can't do it!

For your work attempt to be considered unsuccessful (and therefore, not hurt your case), first, there must be a break in your work activity of at least 30 days. That means that from your onset date – or the date that you became disabled – there must be a break of at least 30 days before you can try going back to work.

Next, the Social Security Administration looks at how long you attempted to work and whether there were any special conditions. If your work attempt lasted for 3 months or less, then it is considered an unsuccessful work attempt when your work ended (or was reduced below the substantial gainful activity limit $1180 for 2018) because of your impairment or because special conditions were removed that allowed you to work.

For example, let's say you go back to work and have to stop after 2 months because you keep showing up late and you are asked to leave; or you were told that you could lie down as needed but your employer wouldn't allow you to lie down after 2 months and you had to stop working. Your 2 month work attempt is considered an "unsuccessful work attempt" and will not hurt your Social Security Disability case.

If your work attempt lasted between 3 and 6 months, then it is considered an unsuccessful work attempt when your work ended (or was reduced below the substantial gainful activity limit $1180 for 2018) because of your impairment or because special conditions were removed that allowed you to work, AND you had one of the following:
- You had frequent absences because of your impairment
- Your work was unsatisfactory because of your impairment
- Your work attempt happened while you were having a temporary remission of your impairment or
- Your work was done under special conditions

*Special Conditions*
A "special condition" is when one of the following things happened

that helped you work:
- You required and received special assistance from other employees to perform your job
- You were allowed to work irregular hours or take frequent rest periods
- You were provided special equipment or were assigned work especially suited to your impairment
- You were able to work only because of a special arrangement, such as people helped you prepare for and get to work
- You were allowed to perform at lower standards of productivity, or
- You only got the job because if a family relationship, friendship, or other charitable reason

What if your work attempt lasts longer than 6 months? A work attempt that is longer than 6 months can hurt your Social Security Disability case. Let's say that you stopped working in January 2014. You went back to work In November 2014 just to see if you could do it. Your work attempt lasted 7 months and you had to stop working in June 2015 because of your impairments. Unfortunately, the Social Security Administration will consider this a successful work attempt! Your onset date – the date that you became disabled – may now be June 2015 and you could lose out on a year's worth of benefits!

If you are considering trying to go back to work, keep these limits and requirements in mind! You don't want a work attempt to hurt your case if you actually can't work!

**Cases that can be Expedited**
Sometimes, you can get your case expedited. The Social Security Administration will flag your case and move it to the front of the line when:

(1)  You have a terminal illness (one that is expected to end

in death)

(2)    You have received a 100% permanent and total disability rating from the Veteran's Administration

(3)    You are a wounded warrior and were injured (physical or mental) while on active duty status

(4)    Your impairment is listed as part of the Compassionate Allowances Program (see Appendix 2)

(5)    You have a dire need and can show: you are without food and unable to obtain it, you lack medicine or medical care and you are unable to obtain it, and/or you lack shelter

(6)    You are suicidal or homicidal

If you have one of these cases, then your case will be expedited. If something changes and when you initially applied, your case did not fit into one of these categories, but now you fit into one of these categories, you will need to let the Social Security Administration know as soon as possible.

As an aside, before you notify the Social Security Administration that your case needs to be expedited, make sure that your medical records are up to date and reflect the level of disability that you are alleging. You don't want to expedite a denial!

### Long Term Disability Insurance
Congratulations! You have been getting paid since the time you went out of work (or very soon after you went out of work). Your Long Term Disability insurance company has likely been gathering your medical records and has been having your doctors fill out forms. Your Long Term Disability company will likely require that you apply for Social Security Disability, and they will send an attorney or non-attorney representative to represent you at your hearing for free!

Here is what's going on and why this is a benefit to you: your Long Term Disability insurance company has likely contracted with another company to help you apply for Social Security Disability.

That company will manage your case from start to finish and coordinate with the insurance company to get your medical records.

The insurance company wants to get you on Social Security Disability so that they can offset for Social Security Disability benefits. What does that mean? The insurance company will subtract what you get from Social Security. That means if you are getting $1,000 from the insurance company each month and then you get approved for Social Security Disability and Social Security is going to pay you $600 per month, that means that your insurance company will then pay you $400 per month. Essentially, your insurance company will make up the difference.

This offset provision will kick in only for the time that Social Security agrees to pay you. That means that if, for example, you went out of work in January 2014, you applied for Social Security Disability in January 2015, and you were approved for benefits in January 2018. In your decision, the judge found you disabled beginning January 2014. There's a 5 month waiting period before you are eligible for benefits, so you are eligible for Social Security Disability benefits beginning June 2014.

So, let's say you get your award letter in January 2018. You would be entitled to back pay from June 2014 until January 2018. That's a big check! Now, let's say that the insurance company was paying you during that time, so January 2014 and January 2018. The insurance company will apply the offset provision from June 2014 to January 2018 as well as for your ongoing payments. So that big check that you will get for backpay? Don't spend it because you will likely have to give most of it back to the insurance company.

You are likely thinking "how is this a benefit to me? I just had to turn over a very large check to the insurance company!" I get it. It's hard to hand over money like that. During the time that you went out of work and had to wait for Social Security, you wouldn't have had any money if it weren't for your insurance company. People without insurance end up having to beg, borrow, and (sometimes) steal to get by while they are waiting for Social Security to (finally) make a decision. So, the real benefit is having that income while you are waiting and perhaps even after if your Social Security Disability benefit is low.

You may also be wondering whether the lawyer they send will be a good one and whether they have even looked at your case. You have probably been communicating with everyone over the phone and no one has ever met you in person. Let me put your fears to rest. The attorney or non-attorney representative that the insurance company sends will likely do Social Security hearings exclusively. I have known many of these attorneys and can say that (at least the ones I've known) they have top-notch training, know their cases, know the law, and are darn good at what they do. Plus, they usually have a large staff behind them who has gathered medical records and submitted documents on your behalf.

Another thing to put your mind at ease: usually, the standard for getting on Long Term Disability is that you are unable to do your job. This should sound familiar to you because it is similar to Step 4 of the Sequential Evaluation Process. At Step 4, Social Security takes it *a little* further in that you must be unable to perform any of your past work 15 years prior to your application. For the most part, people who meet the requirements for their Long Term Disability insurance company usually meet the requirements through Step 4. That is good news!

So, why would you apply for Social Security Disability if you are getting Long Term Disability? Why go through the headache? As I mentioned before, your insurance company will likely require you to apply. Other than that, because you are applying for Title 2 benefits, you will get a disability freeze on your earnings record.

## Disability Freeze

A disability freeze applies only to Title 2 benefits. After you are approved for disability, your earnings record is frozen. That means that the portions of your earnings record during the time that you are disabled are ignored when the Social Security Administration goes to calculate your retirement (or survivors) benefit. So, let's say that you didn't apply for and receive Social Security Disability. Your earnings record would post a "0" for each quarter that you didn't work and pay taxes. Let's also say that this goes on for years. Then, when you go to sign up for Social Security Retirement, your benefit amount is next to nothing because all of those zeros got factored into the total.

Now, let's say that you did apply for and receive Social Security Disability. Your earnings record stops when the Social Security Administration determines that you became disabled. Now, when you go to sign up for Social Security Retirement, your monthly benefit amount is preserved.

Let's say that you become unable to work when you are 61. You apply for Social Security Disability but it is taking quite a long time. Someone from Social Security calls you and asks you if you want to begin getting Social Security Retirement when you turn 62. Your monthly benefit amount is lower than if you wait until you are 65. If you can, resist taking early retirement. Instead, pursue your Social Security Disability case. Once Social Security determines that you are disabled, you will be entitled to monthly benefits AND you will get the disability freeze. Essentially, you are preserving a higher retirement benefit. If you have no possible means of supporting yourself at all and can't even buy food, then by all means, take the early retirement!

## Statements from Friends and Family

I always recommend that you get as many letters from friends and family that you can. The Social Security Administration is required to consider these statements, and I think they go a long way to paint a picture of what your life is *really* like.

If you ask someone to write a statement on your behalf, make sure that the person is very familiar with you. It should describe your life on a daily basis and document your struggles with your impairments. Think of these statements as a sneak peek into your life as it is now.

Here are some tips:

- It should be written from personal knowledge – they should know you and your struggles
- The writer should describe your daily activities to the extent the writer is familiar
- The statement should describe what you used to be able to do and what you can do now. Examples are great, such as: "Johnny used to go fishing twice a week. Now, he spends 2 days in bed per week and can't even cook for himself."
- The writer should tell the truth and not exaggerate
- Describe good days and bad days (i.e. what you can do on a bad day and how often you have 'bad' days)
- Estimate per month (or per week) how many bad days you have
- Explain what the writer helps you with now that you are disabled
- If you have problems remembering things, the writer should put some examples in the statement
- If you have difficulty concentrating or you lose focus, the writer should include examples
- The writer shouldn't write about medical issues because that will be covered in your medical records and by statements from your doctors
- Please ask the writer not to compare your case to Joe

Jones down the street (or anyone else) "who isn't even disabled and got disability in 2 weeks!"

- The statement also shouldn't say that you are "disabled" because that is what Social Security says "is a determination reserved for the Commissioner." It's better to describe your daily activities and what you can't do now. Let the Social Security Administration come to that (very obvious) conclusion!

Finally, have the person print their name, sign, and date the statement.

**What Can I do to help my Disability case?**
So, now you want to know what you can do exactly to help your case!

Here's a list:
(1)  Go to the doctor
(2)  Keep going to the doctor
(3)  Let your doctor know that you are applying or have applied for Social Security Disability; have a conversation about whether your doctor is supportive of your claim
(4)  Take your medication, as prescribed
(5)  Assume that everything that you say to your doctor will end up documented in your medical records; therefore, don't complain about Social Security
(6)  If you experience pain, keep a pain journal and write down when you have pain, how long it lasts, and what precipitates the pain
(7)  Don't go on internet chat boards or public social media posts and write about either Social Security or your abilities/disabilities – assume Social Security will do a search to find out what you've posted!
(8)  If your doctor is supportive of your claim, ask your doctor

to complete a statement (see Appendix 3 for sample forms)
(9)  Go to your Consultative Examination appointments (see Consultative Examination section for tips)
(10) Request your medical records and make sure that your complaints are reflected in your doctor's notes
(11) Get statements from friends and family

## Medicare Eligibility

If you applied for and were approved for Title 2 benefits (yippee! Congratuations!), you are eligible for Medicare 24 months after you are eligible for Social Security Disability.

Remember that 5 month waiting period? That comes into play here. For example, if you went out of work January 2014, you applied for Social Security Disability and were (finally) approved in January 2018, then (because of the 5 month waiting period) you became eligible for Social Security Disability benefits in June 2014. Next, count 24 months from that eligibility date and voila! You have your Medicare eligibility date. In our example, you would be eligible for Medicare beginning June 2016.

There will be a monthly Medicare fee that comes out of your Social Security Disability check. You will be automatically enrolled and there is no separate paperwork that you need to fill out.

It is important to note that Medicare is only available for Title 2 recipients, not Title 16. Title 16 recipients will need to apply for Medicaid, if you haven't already.

*What happens to my private insurance after I get Medicare?*
Great question! Most insurers require you to be on Medicare, if you are eligible. Why? Quite frankly, it saves them money! Your current insurance policy *may* convert into a Medi-Gap policy. That's a policy that covers what Medicare doesn't cover. To be sure, call your insurance provider.

*Will I have to switch doctors?*

Maybe. If your current doctors take Medicare, then you should be fine. If not, you may need to find another doctor. You should call your doctor soon after speaking to your insurance company so that you know what will remain of your current policy.

## Termination

You were approved for Social Security Disability. You've been surviving on your disability payments. Now you get a letter saying that your case is under review. What's going on?

After you are approved for Social Security Disability, the Social Security Administration will periodically review your case. They will request your medical records and if everything remains the same, then your benefits will remain.

You will get a letter advising you that you can continue with your benefits during the review or you can choose to terminate your benefits and, if you are found to be disabled (again), then you will be entitled to back pay. If you are found to be "not disabled," you will have to reimburse the Social Security Administration for the time that they paid you, *if* they paid you during a period of non-disability.

Basically, if they find that you are no longer disabled, they will choose a date (usually tied to your medical records) that they can point to and say that you became better on that particular date. If they were paying you on that date and after that date, then you will have to pay them back.

Before they take away your benefits, though, you are entitled to a hearing. Interestingly, the Social Security Act allows you to have a face-to-face hearing at the Reconsideration level. This is the only time that this happens, and it is done at the State Agency (DDS). If they find that you are "not disabled" any longer, then you are entitled to request a hearing before an Administrative Law Judge, just like a regular case.

During the hearing, the issue will be whether you have had medical improvement AND that medical improvement must be related to your ability to work. They have to show that your Residual Functional Capacity improved to the extent that you can perform any job that exists in the national economy.

Of course, there are exceptions when they don't have to find that you have experienced medical improvement, and here they are:

- you have had vocational training that allows you to engage in substantial gainful activity

- there are new and improved diagnostic techniques that show that your impairment isn't as disabling as it was considered to be when you were initially found to be disabled

- the decision to find you disabled was in error, or

- the determination that you were disabled was fraudulently obtained, you went back to work, you cannot be located, you fail to cooperate with the Social Security Administration, or you fail to follow prescribed treatment that would restore your ability to work

In 2016, 1,349,966 people's Social Security Disability benefits were terminated. Of those, 147,687 no longer met the medical standards and experienced medical improvement.

To avoid getting your benefits terminated, you should continue going to the doctor after you are approved for Social Security Disability. You should continue complying with your doctors' orders. If you find yourself in a situation where you are better, you can attempt to return to work. That's called a Trial Work Period.

If you do get better, then you should notify the Social Security Administration right away. You don't want to be in a situation where you have to pay them back!

**Trial Work Period**
Let's say that you are approved for disability (Congratulations!). You start feeling better and think you may be able to work but don't want your benefits terminated.

A trial work period will let you "try out" working to see if you can do it. If your earnings are above $840 per month in 2017 or $850 per month in 2018, then this will trigger a trial work period.

*How long can I work?*
A trial work period lets you try out working for 9 months in a rolling 60 month period. The 9 month period doesn't have to happen all at once. For example, let's say you tried going back to work but only lasted 3 months, then you have 6 months left on your trial work period in that 60 month timeframe before your benefits will be terminated.

Another example: let's say you tried working but could only work every other month because you literally needed a month to recover. You can do this for 18 months. After 18 months, your earnings record will show 9 months of work activity. Your benefits could be terminated even though you really can't work!

Use those 9 months cautiously because once they are gone..... they are gone and you risk having your benefits terminated.

# APPENDIX 1: LISTINGS OF IMPAIRMENTS

Below is a list of the Listings of Impairments. Keep in mind that this list doesn't include the information in the section that comes before the Listings which is a part of each section.

So, for example, Listing 1.02 references "1.00B2b" – which is in what I like to call the "preamble" to the Listings for the 1.00 Listings. For each section, there is information that you *may* need to know if you find that your impairment potentially meets or equals one of these Listings. In that case, go to https://www.ssa.gov/disability/professionals/bluebook/AdultListings.htm and go to the particular category that applies.

This part is a little dense – my apologies! I suggest you go back and look at the Table of Contents to find a category that you might be in and then go to that section to see if you meet the criteria. I wouldn't read through every one of these, unless you find it interesting!

1.01 Category of Impairments, Musculoskeletal
1.02 Major dysfunction of a joint(s) (due to any cause): Characterized by gross anatomical deformity (e.g., subluxation, contracture, bony or fibrous ankylosis, instability) and chronic joint pain and stiffness with signs of limitation of motion or other abnormal motion of the affected joint(s), and findings on appropriate medically acceptable imaging of joint space narrowing, bony destruction, or ankylosis of the affected joint(s). With:
A. Involvement of one major peripheral weight-bearing joint (i.e., hip, knee, or ankle), resulting in inability to ambulate effectively, as defined in 1.00B2b;
or
B. Involvement of one major peripheral joint in each upper extremity (i.e., shoulder, elbow, or wrist-hand), resulting in inability to perform fine and gross movements effectively, as defined in 1.00B2c.
1.03 Reconstructive surgery or surgical arthrodesis of a major weight-bearing joint, with inability to ambulate effectively, as defined in 1.00B2b, and return to effective ambulation did not occur, or is not expected to occur, within 12 months of onset.
1.04 Disorders of the spine (e.g., herniated nucleus pulposus, spinal arachnoiditis, spinal stenosis, osteoarthritis, degenerative disc disease, facet arthritis, vertebral fracture), resulting in compromise of a nerve root (including

the cauda equina) or the spinal cord. With:

A. Evidence of nerve root compression characterized by neuro-anatomic distribution of pain, limitation of motion of the spine, motor loss (atrophy with associated muscle weakness or muscle weakness) accompanied by sensory or reflex loss and, if there is involvement of the lower back, positive straight-leg raising test (sitting and supine);

or

B. Spinal arachnoiditis, confirmed by an operative note or pathology report of tissue biopsy, or by appropriate medically acceptable imaging, manifested by severe burning or painful dysesthesia, resulting in the need for changes in position or posture more than once every 2 hours;

or

C. Lumbar spinal stenosis resulting in pseudoclaudication, established by findings on appropriate medically acceptable imaging, manifested by chronic nonradicular pain and weakness, and resulting in inability to ambulate effectively, as defined in 1.00B2b.

1.05 Amputation (due to any cause).

A. Both hands; or

or

B. One or both lower extremities at or above the tarsal region, with stump complications resulting in medical inability to use a prosthetic device to ambulate effectively, as defined in 1.00B2b, which have lasted or are expected to last for at least 12 months;

or

C. One hand and one lower extremity at or above the tarsal region, with inability to ambulate effectively, as defined in 1.00B2b; OR

D. Hemipelvectomy or hip disarticulation.

1.06 Fracture of the femur, tibia, pelvis, or one or more of the tarsal bones. With:

A. Solid union not evident on appropriate medically acceptable imaging and not clinically solid;

and

B. Inability to ambulate effectively, as defined in 1.00B2b, and return to effective ambulation did not occur or is not expected to occur within 12 months of onset.

1.07 Fracture of an upper extremity with nonunion of a fracture of the shaft of the humerus, radius, or ulna, under continuing surgical management, as defined in 1.00M, directed toward restoration of functional use of the extremity, and such function was not restored or expected to be restored within 12 months of onset.

1.08 Soft tissue injury (e.g., burns) of an upper or lower extremity, trunk, or face and head, under continuing surgical management, as defined in 1.00M, directed toward the salvage or restoration of major function, and such major function was not restored or expected to be restored within 12 months of onset. Major function of the face and head is described in 1.00O.

2.01 Category of Impairments, Special Senses and Speech

2.02 Loss of central visual acuity. Remaining vision in the better eye after best correction is 20/200 or less.

2.03 Contraction of the visual field in the better eye, with:

A. The widest diameter subtending an angle around the point of fixation no greater than 20 degrees.

OR

B. An MD of 22 decibels or greater, determined by automated static threshold perimetry that measures the central 30 degrees of the visual field (see 2.00A6d).

OR

C. A visual field efficiency of 20 percent or less, determined by kinetic perimetry (see 2.00A7c).

2.04 Loss of visual efficiency, or visual impairment, in the better eye:

A. A visual efficiency percentage of 20 or less after best correction (see 2.00A7d).

OR

B. A visual impairment value of 1.00 or greater after best correction (see 2.00A8d).

2.07 Disturbance of labyrinthine-vestibular function (including Meniere's disease), characterized by a history of frequent attacks of balance disturbance, tinnitus, and progressive loss of hearing. With both A and B:

A. Disturbed function of vestibular labyrinth demonstrated by caloric or other vestibular tests; and

B. Hearing loss established by audiometry.

2.09 Loss of speech due to any cause, with inability to produce by any means speech that can be heard, understood, or sustained.

2.10 Hearing loss not treated with cochlear implantation.

A. An average air conduction hearing threshold of 90 decibels or greater in the better ear and an average bone conduction hearing threshold of 60 decibels

or greater in the better ear (see 2.00B2c).
OR
B. A word recognition score of 40 percent or less in the better ear determined using a standardized list of phonetically balanced monosyllabic words (see 2.00B2e).
2.11 Hearing loss treated with cochlear implantation.
A. Consider under a disability for 1 year after initial implantation.
OR
B. If more than 1 year after initial implantation, a word recognition score of 60 percent or less determined using the HINT (see 2.00B3b).

3.01 Category of Impairments, Respiratory Disorders
3.02 Chronic respiratory disorders due to any cause except CF (for CF, see 3.04) with A, B, C, or D:
A. FEV1 (see 3.00E) less than or equal to the value in Table I-A or I-B for your age, gender, and height without shoes (see 3.00E3a).
Table I - FEV1 Criteria for 3.02A

| Height without shoes (centimeters) < means less than | Height without shoes (inches) < means less than | Table I-A | | Table I-B | |
|---|---|---|---|---|---|
| | | Age 18 to attainment of age 20 | | Age 20 or older | |
| | | Females FEV1 less than or equal to (L, BTPS) | Males FEV1 less than or equal to (L, BTPS) | Females FEV1 less than or equal to (L, BTPS) | Males FEV1 less than or equal to (L, BTPS) |
| <153.0 | <60.25 | 1.20 | 1.45 | 1.05 | 1.20 |
| 153.0 to <159.0 | 60.25 to <62.50 | 1.30 | 1.55 | 1.15 | 1.35 |
| 159.0 to <164.0 | 62.50 to <64.50 | 1.40 | 1.65 | 1.25 | 1.40 |
| 164.0 to <169.0 | 64.50 to <66.50 | 1.45 | 1.75 | 1.35 | 1.50 |
| 169.0 to <174.0 | 66.50 to <68.50 | 1.55 | 1.85 | 1.45 | 1.60 |
| 174.0 to <180.0 | 68.50 to <70.75 | 1.65 | 2.00 | 1.55 | 1.75 |
| 180.0 to <185.0 | 70.75 to <72.75 | 1.75 | 2.10 | 1.65 | 1.85 |
| 185.0 or more | 72.75 or more | 1.80 | 2.15 | 1.70 | 1.90 |

OR

B. FVC (see 3.00E) less than or equal to the value in Table II-A or II-B for your age, gender, and height without shoes (see 3.00E3a).

| Height without shoes (centimeters) < means less than | Height without shoes (inches) < means less than | Table II-A | | Table II-B | |
|---|---|---|---|---|---|
| | | Age 18 to attainment of age 20 | | Age 20 or older | |
| | | Females FVC less than or equal to (L, BTPS) | Males FVC less than or equal to (L, BTPS) | Females FVC less than or equal to (L, BTPS) | Males FVC less than or equal to (L, BTPS) |
| <153.0 | <60.25 | 1.35 | 1.65 | 1.30 | 1.50 |
| 153.0 to <159.0 | 60.25 to <62.50 | 1.50 | 1.80 | 1.40 | 1.65 |
| 159.0 to <164.0 | 62.50 to <64.50 | 1.60 | 1.90 | 1.50 | 1.75 |
| 164.0 to <169.0 | 64.50 to <66.50 | 1.70 | 2.05 | 1.60 | 1.90 |
| 169.0 to <174.0 | 66.50 to <68.50 | 1.80 | 2.20 | 1.70 | 2.00 |
| 174.0 to <180.0 | 68.50 to <70.75 | 1.90 | 2.35 | 1.85 | 2.20 |
| 180.0 to <185.0 | 70.75 to <72.75 | 2.05 | 2.50 | 1.95 | 2.30 |
| 185.0 or more | 72.75 or more | 2.10 | 2.60 | 2.00 | 2.40 |

OR

C. Chronic impairment of gas exchange demonstrated by 1, 2, or 3:

1. Average of two unadjusted, single-breath DLCO measurements (see 3.00F) less than or equal to the value in Table III for your gender and height without shoes (see 3.00F3a); or

Table III - DLCO Criteria for 3.02C1

| Height without shoes (centimeters) < means less than | Height without shoes (inches) < means less than | Females DLCO less than or equal to (mL CO (STPD)/min/mmHg) | Males DLCO less than or equal to (mL CO (STPD)/min/mmHg) |
|---|---|---|---|
| <153.0 | < 60.25 | 8.0 | 9.0 |
| 153.0 to <159.0 | 60.25 to <62.50 | 8.5 | 9.5 |
| 159.0 to <164.0 | 62.50 to <64.50 | 9.0 | 10.0 |
| 164.0 to <169.0 | 64.50 to <66.50 | 9.5 | 10.5 |

| | | | |
|---|---|---|---|
| 169.0 to <174.0 | 66.50 to <68.50 | 10.0 | 11.0 |
| 174.0 to <180.0 | 68.50 to <70.75 | 10.5 | 11.5 |
| 180.0 to <185.0 | 70.75 to <72.75 | 11.0 | 12.0 |
| 185.0 or more | 72.75 or more | 11.5 | 12.5 |

2. Arterial PaO2 and PaCO2 measured concurrently by an ABG test, while at rest or during steady state exercise, breathing room air (see 3.00G3b), less than or equal to the applicable values in Table IV-A, IV-B, or IV-C; or

Tables IV-A, IV-B, and IV-C - ABG Criteria for 3.02C2

Table IV-A

[Applicable at test sites less than 3,000 feet above sea level]

| Arterial PaCO2 (mm Hg) and | Arterial PaO2 less than or equal to (mm Hg) |
|---|---|
| 30 or below | 65 |
| 31 | 64 |
| 32 | 63 |
| 33 | 62 |
| 34 | 61 |
| 35 | 60 |
| 36 | 59 |
| 37 | 58 |
| 38 | 57 |
| 39 | 56 |
| 40 or above | 55 |

Table IV-B

[Applicable at test sites from 3,000 through 6,000 feet above sea level]

| Arterial PaCO2 (mm Hg) and | Arterial PaO2 less than or equal to (mm Hg) |
|---|---|
| 30 or below | 60 |
| 31 | 59 |
| 32 | 58 |
| 33 | 57 |
| 34 | 56 |
| 35 | 55 |
| 36 | 54 |
| 37 | 53 |
| 38 | 52 |
| 39 | 51 |
| 40 or above | 50 |

Table IV-C
[Applicable at test sites over 6,000 feet above sea level]

| Arterial PaCO2 (mm Hg) and | Arterial PaO2 less than or equal to (mm Hg) |
|---|---|
| 30 or below | 55 |
| 31 | 54 |
| 32 | 53 |
| 33 | 52 |
| 34 | 51 |
| 35 | 50 |
| 36 | 49 |
| 37 | 48 |
| 38 | 47 |
| 39 | 46 |
| 40 or above | 45 |

3. SpO2 measured by pulse oximetry (see 3.00H2) either at rest, during a 6MWT, or after a 6MWT, less than or equal to the value in Table V.

Table V - SpO2 Criteria for 3.02C3

| Test site altitude (feet above sea level) | SpO2 less than or equal to |
|---|---|
| Less than 3,000 | 87 percent. |
| 3,000 through 6,000 | 85 percent. |
| Over 6,000 | 83 percent. |

OR

D. Exacerbations or complications requiring three hospitalizations within a 12-month period and at least 30 days apart (the 12-month period must occur within the period we are considering in connection with your application or continuing disability review). Each hospitalization must last at least 48 hours, including hours in a hospital emergency department immediately before the hospitalization.

3.03 Asthma (see 3.00I), with both A and B:
A. FEV1 (see 3.00E1) less than or equal to the value in Table VI-A or VI-B for your age, gender, and height without shoes (see 3.00E3a) measured within the same 12-month period as the hospitalizations in 3.03B.

Table VI - FEV1 Criteria for 3.03A

| Height without shoes | Height without shoes | Table VI-A | Table VI-B |
|---|---|---|---|
| | | Age 18 to attainment of age | Age 20 or older |

| (centimeters) | (inches) | 20 | | | |
| < means<br>less than | < means<br>less than | Females<br>FEV1<br>less than or<br>equal to<br>(L, BTPS) | Males<br>FEV1<br>less than or<br>equal to<br>(L, BTPS) | Females<br>FEV1<br>less than or<br>equal to<br>(L, BTPS) | Males<br>FEV1<br>less than or<br>equal to<br>(L, BTPS) |
|---|---|---|---|---|---|
| <153.0 | <60.25 | 1.65 | 1.90 | 1.45 | 1.60 |
| 153.0 to<br><159.0 | 60.25 to<br><62.50 | 1.75 | 2.05 | 1.55 | 1.75 |
| 159.0 to<br><164.0 | 62.50 to<br><64.50 | 1.85 | 2.15 | 1.65 | 1.90 |
| 164.0 to<br><169.0 | 64.50 to<br><66.50 | 1.95 | 2.30 | 1.75 | 2.00 |
| 169.0 to<br><174.0 | 66.50 to<br><68.50 | 2.05 | 2.45 | 1.85 | 2.15 |
| 174.0 to<br><180.0 | 68.50 to<br><70.75 | 2.20 | 2.60 | 2.00 | 2.30 |
| 180.0 to<br><185.0 | 70.75 to<br><72.75 | 2.35 | 2.75 | 2.10 | 2.45 |
| 185.0 or more | 72.75 or more | 2.40 | 2.85 | 2.20 | 2.55 |

AND

B. Exacerbations or complications requiring three hospitalizations within a 12-month period and at least 30 days apart (the 12-month period must occur within the period we are considering in connection with your application or continuing disability review). Each hospitalization must last at least 48 hours, including hours in a hospital emergency department immediately before the hospitalization. Consider under a disability for 1 year from the discharge date of the last hospitalization; after that, evaluate the residual impairment(s) under 3.03 or another appropriate listing.

3.04 Cystic fibrosis (documented as described in 3.00J2) with A, B, C, D, E, F, or G:

A. FEV1 (see 3.00E) less than or equal to the value in Table VII-A or VII-B for your age, gender, and height without shoes (see 3.00E3a).

Table VII - FEV1 Criteria for 3.04A

| Height without<br>shoes<br>(centimeters)<br>< means | Height without<br>shoes<br>(inches)<br>< means | Table VII-A<br>Age 18 to attainment of<br>age 20 | | Table VII-B<br>Age 20 or older | |
|---|---|---|---|---|---|
| | | Females | Males | Females | Males |

| less than | less than | FEV1 less than or equal to (L, BTPS) | FEV1 less than or equal to (L, BTPS) | FEV1 less than or equal to (L, BTPS) | FEV1 less than or equal to (L, BTPS) |
|---|---|---|---|---|---|
| <153.0 | <60.25 | 1.65 | 1.90 | 1.45 | 1.60 |
| 153.0 to <159.0 | 60.25 to <62.50 | 1.75 | 2.05 | 1.55 | 1.75 |
| 159.0 to <164.0 | 62.50 to <64.50 | 1.85 | 2.15 | 1.65 | 1.90 |
| 164.0 to <169.0 | 64.50 to <66.50 | 1.95 | 2.30 | 1.75 | 2.00 |
| 169.0 to <174.0 | 66.50 to <68.50 | 2.05 | 2.45 | 1.85 | 2.15 |
| 174.0 to <180.0 | 68.50 to <70.75 | 2.20 | 2.60 | 2.00 | 2.30 |
| 180.0 to <185.0 | 70.75 to <72.75 | 2.35 | 2.75 | 2.10 | 2.45 |
| 185.0 or more | 72.75 or more | 2.40 | 2.85 | 2.20 | 2.55 |

OR

B. Exacerbations or complications (see 3.00J3) requiring three hospitalizations of any length within a 12-month period and at least 30 days apart (the 12-month period must occur within the period we are considering in connection with your application or continuing disability review).

OR

C. Spontaneous pneumothorax, secondary to CF, requiring chest tube placement.

OR

D. Respiratory failure (see 3.00N) requiring invasive mechanical ventilation, noninvasive ventilation with BiPAP, or a combination of both treatments, for a continuous period of at least 48 hours, or for a continuous period of at least 72 hours if postoperatively.

OR

E. Pulmonary hemorrhage requiring vascular embolization to control bleeding.

OR

F. SpO2 measured by pulse oximetry (see 3.00H3) either at rest, during a 6MWT, or after a 6MWT, less than or equal to the value in Table VIII, twice within a 12-month period and at least 30 days apart (the 12-month period must occur within the period we are considering in connection with your application or continuing disability review).

Tables VIII - SpO2 Criteria for 3.04F

| Test site altitude (feet above sea level) | SpO2 less than or equal to |
|---|---|
| Less than 3,000 | 89 percent. |

| 3,000 through 6,000 | 87 percent. |
| Over 6,000 | 85 percent. |

OR

G. Two of the following exacerbations or complications (either two of the same or two different, see 3.00J3 and 3.00J4) within a 12-month period (the 12-month period must occur within the period we are considering in connection with your application or continuing disability review):

1. Pulmonary exacerbation requiring 10 consecutive days of intravenous antibiotic treatment.

2. Pulmonary hemorrhage (hemoptysis with more than blood-streaked sputum but not requiring vascular embolization) requiring hospitalization of any length.

3. Weight loss requiring daily supplemental enteral nutrition via a gastrostomy for at least 90 consecutive days or parenteral nutrition via a central venous catheter for at least 90 consecutive days.

4. CFRD requiring daily insulin therapy for at least 90 consecutive days.

3.05 [Reserved]

3.06 [Reserved]

3.07 Bronchiectasis (see 3.00K), documented by imaging (see 3.00D3), with exacerbations or complications requiring three hospitalizations within a 12-month period and at least 30 days apart (the 12-month period must occur within the period we are considering in connection with your application or continuing disability review). Each hospitalization must last at least 48 hours, including hours in a hospital emergency department immediately before the hospitalization.

3.08 [Reserved]

3.09 Chronic pulmonary hypertension due to any cause (see 3.00L) documented by mean pulmonary artery pressure equal to or greater than 40 mm Hg as determined by cardiac catheterization while medically stable (see 3.00E2a).

3.10 [Reserved]

3.11 Lung transplantation (see 3.00M). Consider under a disability for 3 years from the date of the transplant; after that, evaluate the residual impairment(s).

3.12 [Reserved]

3.13 [Reserved]

3.14 Respiratory failure (see 3.00N) resulting from any underlying chronic respiratory disorder except CF (for CF, see 3.04D), requiring invasive mechanical ventilation, noninvasive ventilation with BiPAP, or a combination of both treatments, for a continuous period of at least 48 hours, or for a continuous period of at least 72 hours if postoperatively, twice within a 12-month period and at least 30 days apart (the 12-month period must occur within the period we are considering in connection with your application or continuing disability review).

4.01 Category of Impairments, Cardiovascular System
4.02 Chronic heart failure while on a regimen of prescribed treatment, with symptoms and signs described in 4.00D2. The required level of severity for this impairment is met when the requirements in *both A and B* are satisfied.

A. Medically documented presence of one of the following:

1. Systolic failure (see 4.00D1a(i)), with left ventricular end diastolic dimensions greater than 6.0 cm or ejection fraction of 30 percent or less during a period of stability (not during an episode of acute heart failure); or

2. Diastolic failure (see 4.00D1a(ii)), with left ventricular posterior wall plus septal thickness totaling 2.5 cm or greater on imaging, with an enlarged left atrium greater than or equal to 4.5 cm, with normal or elevated ejection fraction during a period of stability (not during an episode of acute heart failure);

AND
B. Resulting in one of the following:

1. Persistent symptoms of heart failure which very seriously limit the ability to independently initiate, sustain, or complete activities of daily living in an individual for whom an MC, preferably one experienced in the care of patients with cardiovascular disease, has concluded that the performance of an exercise test would present a significant risk to the individual; or

2. Three or more separate episodes of acute congestive heart failure within a consecutive 12-month period (see 4.00A3e), with evidence of fluid retention (see 4.00D2b(ii)) from clinical and imaging assessments at the time of the episodes, requiring acute extended physician intervention such as hospitalization or emergency room treatment for 12 hours or more, separated by periods of stabilization (see 4.00D4c); or

3. Inability to perform on an exercise tolerance test at a workload equivalent to 5 METs or less due to:

a. Dyspnea, fatigue, palpitations, or chest discomfort; or

b. Three or more consecutive premature ventricular contractions (ventricular tachycardia), or increasing frequency of ventricular ectopy with at least 6 premature ventricular contractions per minute; or

c. Decrease of 10 mm Hg or more in systolic pressure below the baseline systolic blood pressure or the preceding systolic pressure measured during exercise (see 4.00D4d) due to left ventricular dysfunction, despite an increase in workload; or

d. Signs attributable to inadequate cerebral perfusion, such as ataxic gait or mental confusion.

4.04 *Ischemic heart disease*, with symptoms due to myocardial ischemia, as described in 4.00E3-4.00E7, while on a regimen of prescribed treatment (see 4.00B3 if there is no regimen of prescribed treatment), with one of the following:

A. Sign-or symptom-limited exercise tolerance test demonstrating at least one of the following manifestations at a workload equivalent to 5 METs or less:

1. Horizontal or downsloping depression, in the absence of digitalis glycoside treatment or hypokalemia, of the ST segment of at least −0.10 millivolts (−1.0 mm) in at least 3 consecutive complexes that are on a level baseline in any lead other than aVR, and depression of at least −0.10 millivolts lasting for at least 1 minute of recovery; or

2. At least 0.1 millivolt (1 mm) ST elevation above resting baseline in non-infarct leads during both exercise and 1 or more minutes of recovery; or

3. Decrease of 10 mm Hg or more in systolic pressure below the baseline blood pressure or the preceding systolic pressure measured during exercise (see 4.00E9e) due to left ventricular dysfunction, despite an increase in workload; or

4. Documented ischemia at an exercise level equivalent to 5 METs or less on appropriate medically acceptable imaging, such as radionuclide perfusion scans or stress echocardiography.

OR
B. Three separate ischemic episodes, each requiring revascularization or not amenable to revascularization (see 4.00E9f), within a consecutive 12-month period (see 4.00A3e).

OR
C. Coronary artery disease, demonstrated by angiography (obtained

independent of Social Security disability evaluation) or other appropriate medically acceptable imaging, and in the absence of a timely exercise tolerance test or a timely normal drug-induced stress test, an MC, preferably one experienced in the care of patients with cardiovascular disease, has concluded that performance of exercise tolerance testing would present a significant risk to the individual, with both 1 and 2:

1. Angiographic evidence showing:

a. 50 percent or more narrowing of a nonbypassed left main coronary artery; or

b. 70 percent or more narrowing of another nonbypassed coronary artery; or

c. 50 percent or more narrowing involving a long (greater than 1 cm) segment of a nonbypassed coronary artery; or

d. 50 percent or more narrowing of at least two nonbypassed coronary arteries; or

e. 70 percent or more narrowing of a bypass graft vessel; and

2. Resulting in very serious limitations in the ability to independently initiate, sustain, or complete activities of daily living.

4.05 *Recurrent arrhythmias*, not related to reversible causes, such as electrolyte abnormalities or digitalis glycoside or antiarrhythmic drug toxicity, resulting in uncontrolled (see 4.00A3f), recurrent (see 4.00A3c) episodes of cardiac syncope or near syncope (see 4.00F3b), despite prescribed treatment (see 4.00B3 if there is no prescribed treatment), and documented by resting or ambulatory (Holter) electrocardiography, or by other appropriate medically acceptable testing, coincident with the occurrence of syncope or near syncope (see 4.00F3c).

4.06 Symptomatic congenital heart disease (cyanotic or acyanotic), documented by appropriate medically acceptable imaging (see 4.00A3d) or cardiac catheterization, with one of the following:

A. Cyanosis at rest, and:

1. Hematocrit of 55 percent or greater; or

2. Arterial O2 saturation of less than 90 percent in room air, or resting arterial PO2 of 60 Torr or less.

OR

B. Intermittent right-to-left shunting resulting in cyanosis on exertion (e.g., Eisenmenger's physiology) and with arterial PO2 of 60 Torr or less at a workload equivalent to 5 METs or less.

OR
C. Secondary pulmonary vascular obstructive disease with pulmonary arterial systolic pressure elevated to at least 70 percent of the systemic arterial systolic pressure.

4.09 Heart transplant. Consider under a disability for 1 year following surgery; thereafter, evaluate residual impairment under the appropriate listing.

4.10 Aneurysm of aorta or major branches, due to any cause (e.g., atherosclerosis, cystic medial necrosis, Marfan syndrome, trauma), demonstrated by appropriate medically acceptable imaging, with dissection not controlled by prescribed treatment (see 4.00H6).

4.11 Chronic venous insufficiency of a lower extremity with incompetency or obstruction of the deep venous system and one of the following:

A. Extensive brawny edema (see 4.00G3) involving at least two-thirds of the leg between the ankle and knee or the distal one-third of the lower extremity between the ankle and hip.

OR
B. Superficial varicosities, stasis dermatitis, and either recurrent ulceration or persistent ulceration that has not healed following at least 3 months of prescribed treatment.

4.12 Peripheral arterial disease, as determined by appropriate medically acceptable imaging (see 4.00A3d, 4.00G2, 4.00G5, and 4.00G6), causing intermittent claudication (see 4.00G1) and one of the following:

A. Resting ankle/brachial systolic blood pressure ratio of less than 0.50.

OR
B. Decrease in systolic blood pressure at the ankle on exercise (see 4.00G7a and 4.00C16-4.00C17) of 50 percent or more of pre-exercise level and requiring 10 minutes or more to return to pre-exercise level.

OR
C. Resting toe systolic pressure of less than 30 mm Hg (see 4.00G7c and 4.00G8).

OR

D. Resting toe/brachial systolic blood pressure ratio of less than 0.40 (see 4.00G7c).

5.01 Category of Impairments, Digestive System

5.02 Gastrointestinal hemorrhaging from any cause, requiring blood transfusion (with or without hospitalization) of at least 2 units of blood per transfusion, and occurring at least three times during a consecutive 6-month period. The transfusions must be at least 30 days apart within the 6-month period. Consider under a disability for 1 year following the last documented transfusion; thereafter, evaluate the residual impairment(s).

5.03-5.04 [Reserved]

5.05 Chronic liver disease, with:

A. Hemorrhaging from esophageal, gastric, or ectopic varices or from portal hypertensive gastropathy, demonstrated by endoscopy, x-ray, or other appropriate medically acceptable imaging, resulting in hemodynamic instability as defined in 5.00D5, and requiring hospitalization for transfusion of at least 2 units of blood. Consider under a disability for 1 year following the last documented transfusion; thereafter, evaluate the residual impairment(s).

OR

B. Ascites or hydrothorax not attributable to other causes, despite continuing treatment as prescribed, present on at least two evaluations at least 60 days apart within a consecutive 6-month period. Each evaluation must be documented by:

1. Paracentesis or thoracentesis; or

2. Appropriate medically acceptable imaging or physical examination and one of the following:

a. Serum albumin of 3.0 g/dL or less; or

b. International Normalized Ratio (INR) of at least 1.5.

OR

C. Spontaneous bacterial peritonitis with peritoneal fluid containing an absolute neutrophil count of at least 250 cells/mm 3.

OR

D. Hepatorenal syndrome as described in 5.00D8, with one of the following:

1. Serum creatinine elevation of at least 2 mg/dL; or

2. Oliguria with 24-hour urine output less than 500 mL; or

3. Sodium retention with urine sodium less than 10 mEq per liter.

OR
E. Hepatopulmonary syndrome as described in 5.00D9, with:

1. Arterial oxygenation (PaO2) on room air of:

a. 60 mm Hg or less, at test sites less than 3000 feet above sea level, or

b. 55 mm Hg or less, at test sites from 3000 to 6000 feet, or

c. 50 mm Hg or less, at test sites above 6000 feet; or

2. Documentation of intrapulmonary arteriovenous shunting by contrast-enhanced echocardiography or macroaggregated albumin lung perfusion scan.

OR
F. Hepatic encephalopathy as described in 5.00D10, with 1 and either 2 or 3:

1. Documentation of abnormal behavior, cognitive dysfunction, changes in mental status, or altered state of consciousness (for example, confusion, delirium, stupor, or coma), present on at least two evaluations at least 60 days apart within a consecutive 6-month period; and

2. History of transjugular intrahepatic portosystemic shunt (TIPS) or any surgical portosystemic shunt: or

3. One of the following occurring on at least two evaluations at least 60 days apart within the same consecutive 6-month period as in F1:

a. Asterixis or other fluctuating physical neurological abnormalities; or

b. Electroencephalogram (EEG) demonstrating triphasic slow wave activity; or

c. Serum albumin of 3.0 g/dL or less; or

d. International Normalized Ratio (INR) of 1.5 or greater.

OR
G. End stage liver disease with SSA CLD scores of 22 or greater calculated as described in 5.00D11. Consider under a disability from at least the date of the first score.

5.06 Inflammatory bowel disease (IBD) documented by endoscopy, biopsy, appropriate medically acceptable imaging, or operative findings with:

A. Obstruction of stenotic areas (not adhesions) in the small intestine or colon with proximal dilatation, confirmed by appropriate medically acceptable imaging or in surgery, requiring hospitalization for intestinal decompression or for surgery, and occurring on at least two occasions at least 60 days apart within a consecutive 6-month period;

OR

B. Two of the following despite continuing treatment as prescribed and occurring within the same consecutive 6-month period:

1. Anemia with hemoglobin of less than 10.0 g/dL, present on at least two evaluations at least 60 days apart; or

2. Serum albumin of 3.0 g/dL or less, present on at least two evaluations at least 60 days apart; or

3. Clinically documented tender abdominal mass palpable on physical examination with abdominal pain or cramping that is not completely controlled by prescribed narcotic medication, present on at least two evaluations at least 60 days apart; or

4. Perineal disease with a draining abscess or fistula, with pain that is not completely controlled by prescribed narcotic medication, present on at least two evaluations at least 60 days apart; or

5. Involuntary weight loss of at least 10 percent from baseline, as computed in pounds, kilograms, or BMI, present on at least two evaluations at least 60 days apart; or

6. Need for supplemental daily enteral nutrition via a gastrostomy or daily parenteral nutrition via a central venous catheter.

5.07 Short bowel syndrome (SBS), due to surgical resection of more than one-half of the small intestine, with dependence on daily parenteral nutrition via a central venous catheter (see 5.00F).

5.08 Weight loss due to any digestive disorder despite continuing treatment as prescribed, with BMI of less than 17.50 calculated on at least two evaluations at least 60 days apart within a consecutive 6-month period.

5.09 Liver transplantation. Consider under a disability for 1 year following the date of transplantation; thereafter, evaluate the residual impairment(s) (see 5.00D12 and 5.00H).

6.01 Category of Impairments, Genitourinary Disorders

6.03 Chronic kidney disease, with chronic hemodialysis or peritoneal dialysis (see 6.00C1).

6.04 Chronic kidney disease, with kidney transplant. Consider under a disability for 1 year following the transplant; thereafter, evaluate the residual impairment (see 6.00C2).

6.05 Chronic kidney disease, with impairment of kidney function, with A and B:

A. Reduced glomerular filtration evidenced by one of the following laboratory findings documented on at least two occasions at least 90 days apart during a consecutive 12-month period:

1. Serum creatinine of 4 mg/dL or greater; or

2. Creatinine clearance of 20 ml/min. or less; or

3. Estimated glomerular filtration rate (eGFR) of 20 ml/min/1.73m 2 or less.

AND

B. One of the following:

1. Renal osteodystrophy (see 6.00C3) with severe bone pain and imaging studies documenting bone abnormalities, such as osteitis fibrosa, osteomalacia, or pathologic fractures; or

2. Peripheral neuropathy (see 6.00C4); or

3. Fluid overload syndrome (see 6.00C5) documented by one of the following:

a. Diastolic hypertension greater than or equal to diastolic blood pressure of 110 mm Hg despite at least 90 consecutive days of prescribed therapy, documented by at least two measurements of diastolic blood pressure at least 90 days apart during a consecutive 12-month period; or

b. Signs of vascular congestion or anasarca (see 6.00C6) despite at least 90 consecutive days of prescribed therapy, documented on at least two occasions at least 90 days apart during a consecutive 12-month period; or

4. Anorexia with weight loss (see 6.00C7) determined by body mass index (BMI) of 18.0 or less, calculated on at least two occasions at least 90 days apart during a consecutive 12-month period.

6.06 Nephrotic syndrome, with A and B:

A. Laboratory findings as described in 1 or 2, documented on at least two occasions at least 90 days apart during a consecutive 12-month period:

1. Proteinuria of 10.0 g or greater per 24 hours; or

2. Serum albumin of 3.0 g/dL or less, and

a. Proteinuria of 3.5 g or greater per 24 hours; or

b. Urine total-protein-to-creatinine ratio of 3.5 or greater.

AND
B. Anasarca (see 6.00C6) persisting for at least 90 days despite prescribed treatment.

6.09 Complications of chronic kidney disease (see 6.00C8) requiring at least three hospitalizations within a consecutive 12-month period and occurring at least 30 days apart. Each hospitalization must last at least 48 hours, including hours in a hospital emergency department immediately before the hospitalization.

7.01 Category of Impairments, Hematological Disorders
7.05 Hemolytic anemias, including sickle cell disease, thalassemia, and their variants (see 7.00C), with:

A. Documented painful (vaso-occlusive) crises requiring parenteral (intravenous or intramuscular) narcotic medication, occurring at least six times within a 12-month period with at least 30 days between crises.

OR

B. Complications of hemolytic anemia requiring at least three hospitalizations within a 12-month period and occurring at least 30 days apart. Each hospitalization must last at least 48 hours, which can include hours in a hospital emergency department or comprehensive sickle cell disease center immediately before the hospitalization (see 7.00C2).

OR

C. Hemoglobin measurements of 7.0 grams per deciliter (g/dL) or less, occurring at least three times within a 12-month period with at least 30 days between measurements.

OR

D. Beta thalassemia major requiring life-long RBC transfusions at least once every 6 weeks to maintain life (see 7.00C4).

7.08 Disorders of thrombosis and hemostasis, including hemophilia and thrombocytopenia (see 7.00D), with complications requiring at least three hospitalizations within a 12-month period and occurring at least 30 days apart. Each hospitalization must last at least 48 hours, which can include hours in a hospital emergency department or comprehensive hemophilia treatment center immediately before the hospitalization (see 7.00D2).

7.10 Disorders of bone marrow failure, including myelodysplastic syndromes, aplastic anemia, granulocytopenia, and myelofibrosis (see 7.00E), with:

A. Complications of bone marrow failure requiring at least three hospitalizations within a 12-month period and occurring at least 30 days apart. Each hospitalization must last at least 48 hours, which can include hours in a hospital emergency department immediately before the hospitalization (see 7.00E2).

OR

B. Myelodysplastic syndromes or aplastic anemias requiring life-long RBC transfusions at least once every 6 weeks to maintain life (see 7.00E3).

7.17 Hematological disorders treated by bone marrow or stem cell transplantation (see 7.00F). Consider under a disability for at least 12 consecutive months from the date of transplantation. After that, evaluate any residual impairment(s) under the criteria for the affected body system.

7.18 Repeated complications of hematological disorders (see 7.00G2), including those complications listed in 7.05, 7.08, and 7.10 but without the requisite findings for those listings, or other complications (for example, anemia, osteonecrosis, retinopathy, skin ulcers, silent central nervous system infarction, cognitive or other mental limitation, or limitation of joint movement), resulting in significant, documented symptoms or signs (for example, pain, severe fatigue, malaise, fever, night sweats, headaches, joint or muscle swelling, or shortness of breath), and one of the following at the marked level (see 7.00G4):

A. Limitation of activities of daily living (see 7.00G5).

B. Limitation in maintaining social functioning (see 7.00G6).

C. Limitation in completing tasks in a timely manner due to deficiencies in concentration, persistence, or pace (see 7.00G7).

8.01 Category of Impairments, Skin Disorders

8.02 Ichthyosis, with extensive skin lesions that persist for at least 3 months despite continuing treatment as prescribed.

8.03 Bullous disease (for example, pemphigus, erythema multiforme bullosum, epidermolysis bullosa, bullous pemphigoid, dermatitis herpetiformis), with extensive skin lesions that persist for at least 3 months despite continuing treatment as prescribed.

8.04 Chronic infections of the skin or mucous membranes, with extensive fungating or extensive ulcerating skin lesions that persist for at least 3 months despite continuing treatment as prescribed.

8.05 Dermatitis (for example, psoriasis, dyshidrosis, atopic dermatitis, exfoliative dermatitis, allergic contact dermatitis), with extensive skin lesions that persist for at least 3 months despite continuing treatment as prescribed.

8.06 Hidradenitis suppurativa, with extensive skin lesions involving both axillae, both inguinal areas or the perineum that persist for at least 3 months despite continuing treatment as prescribed.

8.07 Genetic photosensitivity disorders, established as described in 8.00E.

A. Xeroderma pigmentosum. Consider the individual disabled from birth.

B. Other genetic photosensitivity disorders, with:

1. Extensive skin lesions that have lasted or can be expected to last for a continuous period of at least 12 months, or

2. Inability to function outside of a highly protective environment for a continuous period of at least 12 months (see 8.00E2).

8.08 Burns, with extensive skin lesions that have lasted or can be expected to last for a continuous period of at least 12 months (see 8.00F).

9.00 Endocrine Disorders
A. *What is an endocrine disorder?*

An endocrine disorder is a medical condition that causes a hormonal imbalance. When an endocrine gland functions abnormally, producing either too much of a specific hormone (hyperfunction) or too little (hypofunction), the hormonal imbalance can cause various complications in the body. The major glands of the endocrine system are the pituitary, thyroid, parathyroid, adrenal, and pancreas.

B. *How do we evaluate the effects of endocrine disorders?* We evaluate impairments that result from endocrine disorders under the listings for other body systems. For example:

1. *Pituitary gland disorders* can disrupt hormone production and normal functioning in other endocrine glands and in many body systems. The effects of pituitary gland disorders vary depending on which hormones are involved. For example, when pituitary hypofunction affects water and electrolyte balance in the kidney and leads to diabetes insipidus, we evaluate the effects of recurrent dehydration under 6.00.

2. *Thyroid gland disorders* affect the sympathetic nervous system and normal metabolism. We evaluate thyroid-related changes in blood pressure and heart rate that cause arrhythmias or other cardiac dysfunction under 4.00; thyroid-related weight loss under 5.00; hypertensive cerebrovascular accidents (strokes) under 11.00; and cognitive limitations, mood disorders, and anxiety under 12.00.

3. *Parathyroid gland disorders* affect calcium levels in bone, blood, nerves, muscle, and other body tissues. We evaluate parathyroid-related osteoporosis and fractures under 1.00; abnormally elevated calcium levels in the blood (hypercalcemia) that lead to cataracts under 2.00; kidney failure under 6.00; and recurrent abnormally low blood calcium levels (hypocalcemia) that lead to increased excitability of nerves and muscles, such as tetany and muscle spasms, under 11.00.

4. *Adrenal gland disorders* affect bone calcium levels, blood pressure, metabolism, and mental status. We evaluate adrenal-related osteoporosis with fractures that compromises the ability to walk or to use the upper extremities under 1.00; adrenal-related hypertension that worsens heart failure or causes recurrent arrhythmias under 4.00; adrenal-related weight loss under 5.00; and mood disorders under 12.00.

5. *Diabetes mellitus and other pancreatic gland disorders* disrupt the production of several hormones, including insulin, that regulate metabolism and digestion. Insulin is essential to the absorption of glucose from the bloodstream into body cells for conversion into cellular energy. The most common pancreatic gland disorder is *diabetes mellitus* (DM). There are two major types of DM: type 1 and type 2. Both type 1 and type 2 DM are chronic disorders that can have serious disabling complications that meet the duration requirement. Type 1 DM - previously known as "juvenile diabetes" or "insulin-dependent diabetes mellitus" (IDDM) - is an absolute deficiency of insulin production that commonly begins in childhood and continues throughout

adulthood. Treatment of type 1 DM always requires lifelong daily insulin. With type 2 DM - previously known as "adult-onset diabetes mellitus" or "non-insulin-dependent diabetes mellitus" (NIDDM) - the body's cells resist the effects of insulin, impairing glucose absorption and metabolism. Treatment of type 2 DM generally requires lifestyle changes, such as increased exercise and dietary modification, and sometimes insulin in addition to other medications. While both type 1 and type 2 DM are usually controlled, some persons do not achieve good control for a variety of reasons including, but not limited to, hypoglycemia unawareness, other disorders that can affect blood glucose levels, inability to manage DM due to a mental disorder, or inadequate treatment.

a. *Hyperglycemia.* Both types of DM cause hyperglycemia, which is an abnormally high level of blood glucose that may produce acute and long-term complications. Acute complications of hyperglycemia include diabetic ketoacidosis. Long-term complications of chronic hyperglycemia include many conditions affecting various body systems.

> (i) *Diabetic ketoacidosis (DKA).* DKA is an acute, potentially life-threatening complication of DM in which the chemical balance of the body becomes dangerously hyperglycemic and acidic. It results from a severe insulin deficiency, which can occur due to missed or inadequate daily insulin therapy or in association with an acute illness. It usually requires hospital treatment to correct the acute complications of dehydration, electrolyte imbalance, and insulin deficiency. You may have serious complications resulting from your treatment, which we evaluate under the affected body system. For example, we evaluate cardiac arrhythmias under 4.00, intestinal necrosis under 5.00, and cerebral edema and seizures under 11.00. Recurrent episodes of DKA may result from mood or eating disorders, which we evaluate under 12.00.

> (ii) *Chronic hyperglycemia.* Chronic hyperglycemia, which is longstanding abnormally high levels of blood glucose, leads to long-term diabetic complications by disrupting nerve and blood vessel functioning. This disruption can have many different effects in other body systems. For example, we evaluate diabetic peripheral neurovascular disease that leads to gangrene and subsequent amputation of an extremity under 1.00; diabetic retinopathy under 2.00; coronary artery disease and peripheral vascular disease under 4.00; diabetic gastroparesis that results in abnormal gastrointestinal motility under 5.00; diabetic nephropathy under 6.00; poorly healing bacterial and fungal skin

infections under 8.00; diabetic peripheral and sensory neuropathies under 11.00; and cognitive impairments, depression, and anxiety under 12.00.

b. *Hypoglycemia.* Persons with DM may experience episodes of hypoglycemia, which is an abnormally low level of blood glucose. Most adults recognize the symptoms of hypoglycemia and reverse them by consuming substances containing glucose; however, some do not take this step because of hypoglycemia unawareness. Severe hypoglycemia can lead to complications, including seizures or loss of consciousness, which we evaluate under 11.00, or altered mental status and cognitive deficits, which we evaluate under 12.00.

C. *How do we evaluate endocrine disorders that do not have effects that meet or medically equal the criteria of any listing in other body systems?* If your impairment(s) does not meet or medically equal a listing in another body system, you may or may not have the residual functional capacity to engage in substantial gainful activity. In this situation, we proceed to the fourth and, if necessary, the fifth steps of the sequential evaluation process in §§ 404.1520 and 416.920. When we decide whether you continue to be disabled, we use the rules in §§ 404.1594, 416.994, and 416.994a.

10.01 Category of Impairments, Congenital Disorders That Affect Multiple Body Systems
10.06 Non-mosaic Down syndrome (chromosome 21 trisomy or chromosome 21 translocation), documented by:

A. A laboratory report of karyotype analysis signed by a physician, or both a laboratory report of karyotype analysis not signed by a physician *and* a statement by a physician that you have Down syndrome (see 10.00C1), or

B. A physician's report stating that you have chromosome 21 trisomy or chromosome 21 translocation consistent with prior karyotype analysis with the distinctive facial or other physical features of Down syndrome (see 10.00C2a), or

C. A physician's report stating that you have Down syndrome with the distinctive facial or other physical features *and* evidence demonstrating that you function at a level consistent with non-mosaic Down syndrome (see 10.00C2b).

11.01 Category of Impairments, Neurological Disorders

11.02 Epilepsy, documented by a detailed description of a typical seizure and characterized by A, B, C, or D:

A. Generalized tonic-clonic seizures (see 11.00H1a), occurring at least once a month for at least 3 consecutive months (see 11.00H4) despite adherence to prescribed treatment (see 11.00C); or

B. Dyscognitive seizures (see 11.00H1b), occurring at least once a week for at least 3 consecutive months (see 11.00H4) despite adherence to prescribed treatment (see 11.00C); or

C. Generalized tonic-clonic seizures (see 11.00H1a), occurring at least once every 2 months for at least 4 consecutive months (see 11.00H4) despite adherence to prescribed treatment (see 11.00C); and a marked limitation in one of the following:

1. Physical functioning (see 11.00G3a); or

2. Understanding, remembering, or applying information (see 11.00G3b(i)); or

3. Interacting with others (see 11.00G3b(ii)); or

4. Concentrating, persisting, or maintaining pace (see 11.00G3b(iii)); or

5. Adapting or managing oneself (see 11.00G3b(iv)); or

D. Dyscognitive seizures (see 11.00H1b), occurring at least once every 2 weeks for at least 3 consecutive months (see 11.00H4) despite adherence to prescribed treatment (see 11.00C); and a marked limitation in one of the following:

1. Physical functioning (see 11.00G3a); or

2. Understanding, remembering, or applying information (see 11.00G3b(i)); or

3. Interacting with others (see 11.00G3b(ii)); or

4. Concentrating, persisting, or maintaining pace (see 11.00G3b(iii)); or

5. Adapting or managing oneself (see 11.00G3b(iv)).

11.03 [Reserved]
11.04 Vascular insult to the brain, characterized by A, B, or C:

A. Sensory or motor aphasia resulting in ineffective speech or communication (see 11.00E1) persisting for at least 3 consecutive months after the insult; or

B. Disorganization of motor function in two extremities (see 11.00D1), resulting in an extreme limitation (see 11.00D2) in the ability to stand up from a seated position, balance while standing or walking, or use the upper extremities, persisting for at least 3 consecutive months after the insult; or

C. Marked limitation (see 11.00G2) in physical functioning (see 11.00G3a) and in one of the following areas of mental functioning, both persisting for at least 3 consecutive months after the insult:

1. Understanding, remembering, or applying information (see 11.00G3b(i)); or

2. Interacting with others (see 11.00G3b(ii)); or

3. Concentrating, persisting, or maintaining pace (see 11.00G3b(iii)); or

4. Adapting or managing oneself (see 11.00G3b(iv)).

11.05  Benign brain tumors, characterized by A or B:

A. Disorganization of motor function in two extremities (see 11.00D1), resulting in an extreme limitation (see 11.00D2) in the ability to stand up from a seated position, balance while standing or walking, or use the upper extremities; or

B. Marked limitation (see 11.00G2) in physical functioning (see 11.00G3a), and in one of the following:

1. Understanding, remembering, or applying information (see 11.00G3b(i)); or

2. Interacting with others (see 11.00G3b(ii)); or

3. Concentrating, persisting, or maintaining pace (see 11.00G3b(iii)); or

4. Adapting or managing oneself (see 11.00G3b(iv)).

11.06  Parkinsonian syndrome, characterized by A or B despite adherence to prescribed treatment for at least 3 consecutive months (see 11.00C):

A. Disorganization of motor function in two extremities (see 11.00D1), resulting in an extreme limitation (see 11.00D2) in the ability to stand up from a seated position, balance while standing or walking, or use the upper extremities; or

B. Marked limitation (see 11.00G2) in physical functioning (see 11.00G3a), and in one of the following:

1. Understanding, remembering, or applying information (see 11.00G3b(i)); or

2. Interacting with others (see 11.00G3b(ii)); or

3. Concentrating, persisting, or maintaining pace (see 11.00G3b(iii)); or

4. Adapting or managing oneself (see 11.00G3b(iv)).

11.07  Cerebral palsy, characterized by A, B, or C:

A. Disorganization of motor function in two extremities (see 11.00D1), resulting in an extreme limitation (see 11.00D2) in the ability to stand up from a seated position, balance while standing or walking, or use the upper extremities; or

B. Marked limitation (see 11.00G2) in physical functioning (see 11.00G3a), and in one of the following:

1. Understanding, remembering, or applying information (see 11.00G3b(i)); or

2. Interacting with others (see 11.00G3b(ii)); or

3. Concentrating, persisting, or maintaining pace (see 11.00G3b(iii)); or

4. Adapting or managing oneself (see 11.00G3b(iv)); or

C. Significant interference in communication due to speech, hearing, or visual deficit (see 11.00E2).

11.08  Spinal cord disorders, characterized by A, B, or C:

A. Complete loss of function, as described in 11.00M2, persisting for 3 consecutive months after the disorder (see 11.00M4); or

B. Disorganization of motor function in two extremities (see 11.00D1), resulting in an extreme limitation (see 11.00D2) in the ability to stand up from a seated position, balance while standing or walking, or use the upper extremities persisting for 3 consecutive months after the disorder (see 11.00M4); or

C. Marked limitation (see 11.00G2) in physical functioning (see 11.00G3a) and in one of the following areas of mental functioning, both persisting for 3 consecutive months after the disorder (see 11.00M4):

1. Understanding, remembering, or applying information (see 11.00G3b(i)); or

2. Interacting with others (see 11.00G3b(ii)); or

3. Concentrating, persisting, or maintaining pace (see 11.00G3b(iii)); or

4. Adapting or managing oneself (see 11.00G3b(iv)).

11.09 Multiple sclerosis, characterized by A or B:

A. Disorganization of motor function in two extremities (see 11.00D1), resulting in an extreme limitation (see 11.00D2) in the ability to stand up from a seated position, balance while standing or walking, or use the upper extremities; or

B. Marked limitation (see 11.00G2) in physical functioning (see 11.00G3a), and in one of the following:

1. Understanding, remembering, or applying information (see 11.00G3b(i)); or

2. Interacting with others (see 11.00G3b(ii)); or

3. Concentrating, persisting, or maintaining pace (see 11.00G3b(iii)); or

4. Adapting or managing oneself (see 11.00G3b(iv)).

11.10 Amyotrophic lateral sclerosis (ALS) established by clinical and laboratory findings (see 11.00O).

11.11 Post-polio syndrome, characterized by A, B, C, or D:

A. Disorganization of motor function in two extremities (see 11.00D1), resulting in an extreme limitation (see 11.00D2) in the ability to stand up from a seated position, balance while standing or walking, or use the upper extremities; or

B. Unintelligible speech (see 11.00E3); or

C. Bulbar and neuromuscular dysfunction (see 11.00F), resulting in:

1. Acute respiratory failure requiring mechanical ventilation; or

2. Need for supplemental enteral nutrition via a gastrostomy or parenteral nutrition via a central venous catheter; or

D. Marked limitation (see 11.00G2) in physical functioning (see 11.00G3a), and in one of the following:

1. Understanding, remembering, or applying information (see 11.00G3b(i)); or

2. Interacting with others (see 11.00G3b(ii)); or

3. Concentrating, persisting, or maintaining pace (see 11.00G3b(iii)); or

4. Adapting or managing oneself (see 11.00G3b(iv)).

11.12 Myasthenia gravis, characterized by A, B, or C despite adherence to prescribed treatment for at least 3 months (see 11.00C):

A. Disorganization of motor function in two extremities (see 11.00D1), resulting in an extreme limitation (see 11.00D2) in the ability to stand up from a seated position, balance while standing or walking, or use the upper extremities; or

B. Bulbar and neuromuscular dysfunction (see 11.00F), resulting in:

1. One myasthenic crisis requiring mechanical ventilation; or

2. Need for supplemental enteral nutrition via a gastrostomy or parenteral nutrition via a central venous catheter; or

C. Marked limitation (see 11.00G2) in physical functioning (see 11.00G3a), and in one of the following:

1. Understanding, remembering, or applying information (see 11.00G3b(i)); or

2. Interacting with others (see 11.00G3b(ii)); or

3. Concentrating, persisting, or maintaining pace (see 11.00G3b(iii)); or

4. Adapting or managing oneself (see 11.00G3b(iv)).

11.13 Muscular dystrophy, characterized by A or B:

A. Disorganization of motor function in two extremities (see 11.00D1), resulting in an extreme limitation (see 11.00D2) in the ability to stand up from a seated position, balance while standing or walking, or use the upper extremities; or

B. Marked limitation (see 11.00G2) in physical functioning (see 11.00G3a), and in one of the following:

1. Understanding, remembering, or applying information (see 11.00G3b(i)); or

2. Interacting with others (see 11.00G3b(ii)); or

3. Concentrating, persisting, or maintaining pace (see 11.00G3b(iii)); or

4. Adapting or managing oneself (see 11.00G3b(iv)).

11.14 Peripheral neuropathy, characterized by A or B:

A. Disorganization of motor function in two extremities (see 11.00D1), resulting in an extreme limitation (see 11.00D2) in the ability to stand up from a seated position, balance while standing or walking, or use the upper extremities; or

B. Marked limitation (see 11.00G2) in physical functioning (see 11.00G3a), and in one of the following:

1. Understanding, remembering, or applying information (see 11.00G3b(i)); or

2. Interacting with others (see 11.00G3b(ii)); or

3. Concentrating, persisting, or maintaining pace (see 11.00G3b(iii)); or

4. Adapting or managing oneself (see 11.00G3b(iv)).

11.15 [Reserved]

11.16 [Reserved]

11.17 Neurodegenerative disorders of the central nervous system, *such as Huntington's disease, Friedreich's ataxia, and spinocerebellar degeneration,* characterized by A or B:

A. Disorganization of motor function in two extremities (see 11.00D1), resulting in an extreme limitation (see 11.00D2) in the ability to stand up from a seated position, balance while standing or walking, or use the upper extremities; or

B. Marked limitation (see 11.00G2) in physical functioning (see 11.00G3a), and in one of the following:

1. Understanding, remembering, or applying information (see 11.00G3b(i)); or

2. Interacting with others (see 11.00G3b(ii)); or

3. Concentrating, persisting, or maintaining pace (see 11.00G3b(iii)); or

4. Adapting or managing oneself (see 11.00G3b(iv)).

11.18 Traumatic brain injury, characterized by A or B:

A. Disorganization of motor function in two extremities (see 11.00D1), resulting in an extreme limitation (see 11.00D2) in the ability to stand up from a seated position, balance while standing or walking, or use the upper extremities, persisting for at least 3 consecutive months after the injury; or

B. Marked limitation (see 11.00G2) in physical functioning (see 11.00G3a), and in one of the following areas of mental functioning, persisting for at least 3 consecutive months after the injury:

1. Understanding, remembering, or applying information (see 11.00G3b(i)); or

2. Interacting with others (see 11.00G3b(ii)); or

3. Concentrating, persisting, or maintaining pace (see 11.00G3b(iii)); or

4. Adapting or managing oneself (see 11.00G3b(iv)).

11.19 [Reserved]
11.20 Coma or persistent vegetative state, persisting for at least 1 month.

11.21 [Reserved]
11.22 Motor neuron disorders other than ALS, characterized by A, B, or C:

A. Disorganization of motor function in two extremities (see 11.00D1), resulting in an extreme limitation (see 11.00D2) in the ability to stand up from a seated position, balance while standing or walking, or use the upper extremities; or

B. Bulbar and neuromuscular dysfunction (see 11.00F), resulting in:

1. Acute respiratory failure requiring invasive mechanical ventilation; or

2. Need for supplemental enteral nutrition via a gastrostomy or parenteral nutrition via a central venous catheter; or

C. Marked limitation (see 11.00G2) in physical functioning (see 11.00G3a), and in one of the following:

1. Understanding, remembering, or applying information (see 11.00G3b(i)); or

2. Interacting with others (see 11.00G3b(ii)); or

3. Concentrating, persisting, or maintaining pace (see 11.00G3b(iii)); or

4. Adapting or managing oneself (see 11.00G3b(iv)).

12.01 Category of Impairments, Mental Disorders
12.02 Neurocognitive disorders (see 12.00B1), satisfied by A and B, or A and C:

A. Medical documentation of a significant cognitive decline from a prior level of functioning in *one* or more of the cognitive areas:

1. Complex attention;

2. Executive function;

3. Learning and memory;

4. Language;

5. Perceptual-motor; or

6. Social cognition.

**AND**
B. Extreme limitation of one, or marked limitation of two, of the following areas of mental functioning (see 12.00F):

1. Understand, remember, or apply information (see 12.00E1).

2. Interact with others (see 12.00E2).

3. Concentrate, persist, or maintain pace (see 12.00E3).

4. Adapt or manage oneself (see 12.00E4).

**OR**
C. Your mental disorder in this listing category is "serious and persistent;" that is, you have a medically documented history of the existence of the disorder over a period of at least 2 years, and there is evidence of both:

*1.* Medical treatment, mental health therapy, psychosocial support(s), or a highly structured setting(s) that is ongoing and that diminishes the symptoms and signs of your mental disorder (see 12.00G2b); *and*

2. Marginal adjustment, that is, you have minimal capacity to adapt to changes in your environment or to demands that are not already part of your daily life (see 12.00G2c).

12.03 *Schizophrenia spectrum and other psychotic disorders* (see 12.00B2), satisfied by A and B, or A and C:

A. Medical documentation of *one* or more of the following:

1. Delusions or hallucinations;

2. Disorganized thinking (speech); or

3. Grossly disorganized behavior or catatonia.

**AND**
B. Extreme limitation of one, or marked limitation of two, of the following areas of mental functioning (see 12.00F):

1. Understand, remember, or apply information (see 12.00E1).

2. Interact with others (see 12.00E2).

3. Concentrate, persist, or maintain pace (see 12.00E3).

4. Adapt or manage oneself (see 12.00E4).

**OR**

C. Your mental disorder in this listing category is "serious and persistent;" that is, you have a medically documented history of the existence of the disorder over a period of at least 2 years, and there is evidence of both:

*1.* Medical treatment, mental health therapy, psychosocial support(s), or a highly structured setting(s) that is ongoing and that diminishes the symptoms and signs of your mental disorder (see 12.00G2b); *and*

2. Marginal adjustment, that is, you have minimal capacity to adapt to changes in your environment or to demands that are not already part of your daily life (see 12.00G2c).

12.04 Depressive, bipolar and related disorders (see 12.00B3), satisfied by A and B, or A and C:

A. Medical documentation of the requirements of paragraph 1 or 2:

1. Depressive disorder, characterized by *five* or more of the following:

a. Depressed mood;

b. Diminished interest in almost all activities;

c. Appetite disturbance with change in weight;

d. Sleep disturbance;

e. Observable psychomotor agitation or retardation;

f. Decreased energy;

g. Feelings of guilt or worthlessness;

h. Difficulty concentrating or thinking; or

i. Thoughts of death or suicide.

2. Bipolar disorder, characterized by *three* or more of the following:

a. Pressured speech;

b. Flight of ideas;

c. Inflated self-esteem;

d. Decreased need for sleep;

e. Distractibility;

f. Involvement in activities that have a high probability of painful consequences that are not recognized; or

g. Increase in goal-directed activity or psychomotor agitation.

**AND**
B. Extreme limitation of one, or marked limitation of two, of the following areas of mental functioning (see 12.00F):

1. Understand, remember, or apply information (see 12.00E1).

2. Interact with others (see 12.00E2).

3. Concentrate, persist, or maintain pace (see 12.00E3).

4. Adapt or manage oneself (see 12.00E4).

**OR**
C. Your mental disorder in this listing category is "serious and persistent;" that is, you have a medically documented history of the existence of the disorder over a period of at least 2 years, and there is evidence of both:

*1.* Medical treatment, mental health therapy, psychosocial support(s), or a highly structured setting(s) that is ongoing and that diminishes the symptoms and signs of your mental disorder (see 12.00G2b); *and*

2. Marginal adjustment, that is, you have minimal capacity to adapt to changes in your environment or to demands that are not already part of your daily life (see 12.00G2c).

12.05 Intellectual disorder (see 12.00B4), satisfied by A or B:

A. Satisfied by 1, 2, and 3 (see 12.00H):

1. Significantly subaverage general intellectual functioning evident in your cognitive inability to function at a level required to participate in standardized testing of intellectual functioning; and

2. Significant deficits in adaptive functioning currently manifested by your dependence upon others for personal needs (for example, toileting, eating, dressing, or bathing); and

3. The evidence about your current intellectual and adaptive functioning and about the history of your disorder demonstrates or supports the conclusion that the disorder began prior to your attainment of age 22.

**OR**

B. Satisfied by 1, 2, and 3 (see 12.00H):

1. Significantly subaverage general intellectual functioning evidenced by a or b:

a. A full scale (or comparable) IQ score of 70 or below on an individually administered standardized test of general intelligence; or

b. A full scale (or comparable) IQ score of 71-75 accompanied by a verbal or performance IQ score (or comparable part score) of 70 or below on an individually administered standardized test of general intelligence; and

2. Significant deficits in adaptive functioning currently manifested by extreme limitation of one, or marked limitation of two, of the following areas of mental functioning:

a. Understand, remember, or apply information (see 12.00E1); or

b. Interact with others (see 12.00E2); or

c. Concentrate, persist, or maintain pace (see 12.00E3); or

d. Adapt or manage oneself (see 12.00E4); and

3. The evidence about your current intellectual and adaptive functioning and about the history of your disorder demonstrates or supports the conclusion that the disorder began prior to your attainment of age 22.

12.06 Anxiety and obsessive-compulsive disorders (see 12.00B5), satisfied by A and B, or A and C:

A. Medical documentation of the requirements of paragraph 1, 2, or 3:

1. Anxiety disorder, characterized by *three* or more of the following;

a. Restlessness;

b. Easily fatigued;

c. Difficulty concentrating;

d. Irritability;

e. Muscle tension; or

f. Sleep disturbance.

2. Panic disorder or agoraphobia, characterized by *one* or both:

a. Panic attacks followed by a persistent concern or worry about additional panic attacks or their consequences; or

b. Disproportionate fear or anxiety about at least two different situations (for example, using public transportation, being in a crowd, being in a line, being outside of your home, being in open spaces).

3. Obsessive-compulsive disorder, characterized by *one* or both:

a. Involuntary, time-consuming preoccupation with intrusive, unwanted thoughts; or

b. Repetitive behaviors aimed at reducing anxiety.

**AND**
B. Extreme limitation of one, or marked limitation of two, of the following areas of mental functioning (see 12.00F):

1. Understand, remember, or apply information (see 12.00E1).

2. Interact with others (see 12.00E2).

3. Concentrate, persist, or maintain pace (see 12.00E3).

4. Adapt or manage oneself (see 12.00E4).

**OR**
C. Your mental disorder in this listing category is "serious and persistent;" that is, you have a medically documented history of the existence of the disorder over a period of at least 2 years, and there is evidence of both:

*1.* Medical treatment, mental health therapy, psychosocial support(s), or a highly structured setting(s) that is ongoing and that diminishes the symptoms and signs of your mental disorder (see 12.00G2b); *and*

2. Marginal adjustment, that is, you have minimal capacity to adapt to changes in your environment or to demands that are not already part of your daily life (see 12.00G2c).

12.07 Somatic symptom and related disorders (see 12.00B6), satisfied by A and B:

A. Medical documentation of *one* or more of the following:

1. Symptoms of altered voluntary motor or sensory function that are not better explained by another medical or mental disorder;

2. One or more somatic symptoms that are distressing, with excessive thoughts, feelings, or behaviors related to the symptoms; or

3. Preoccupation with having or acquiring a serious illness without significant symptoms present.

**AND**

B. Extreme limitation of one, or marked limitation of two, of the following areas of mental functioning (see 12.00F):

1. Understand, remember, or apply information (see 12.00E1).

2. Interact with others (see 12.00E2).

3. Concentrate, persist, or maintain pace (see 12.00E3).

4. Adapt or manage oneself (see 12.00E4).

12.08 Personality and impulse-control disorders (see 12.00B7), satisfied by A and B:

A. Medical documentation of a pervasive pattern of *one* or more of the following:

1. Distrust and suspiciousness of others;

2. Detachment from social relationships;

3. Disregard for and violation of the rights of others;

4. Instability of interpersonal relationships;

5. Excessive emotionality and attention seeking;

6. Feelings of inadequacy;

7. Excessive need to be taken care of;

8. Preoccupation with perfectionism and orderliness; or

9. Recurrent, impulsive, aggressive behavioral outbursts.

**AND**

B. Extreme limitation of one, or marked limitation of two, of the following areas of mental functioning (see 12.00F):

1. Understand, remember, or apply information (see 12.00E1).

2. Interact with others (see 12.00E2).

3. Concentrate, persist, or maintain pace (see 12.00E3).

4. Adapt or manage oneself (see 12.00E4).

12.09 [Reserved]

12.10 *Autism spectrum disorder* (see 12.00B8), satisfied by A and B:

A. Medical documentation of *both* of the following:

1. Qualitative deficits in verbal communication, nonverbal communication, and social interaction; and

2. Significantly restricted, repetitive patterns of behavior, interests, or activities.

**AND**
B. Extreme limitation of one, or marked limitation of two, of the following areas of mental functioning (see 12.00F):

1. Understand, remember, or apply information (see 12.00E1).

2. Interact with others (see 12.00E2).

3. Concentrate, persist, or maintain pace (see 12.00E3).

4. Adapt or manage oneself (see 12.00E4).

12.11 Neurodevelopmental disorders (see 12.00B9), satisfied by A and B:

A. Medical documentation of the requirements of paragraph 1, 2, or 3:

1. *One* or both of the following:

a. Frequent distractibility, difficulty sustaining attention, and difficulty organizing tasks; or

b. Hyperactive and impulsive behavior (for example, difficulty remaining seated, talking excessively, difficulty waiting, appearing restless, or behaving as if being "driven by a motor").

2. Significant difficulties learning and using academic skills; or

3. Recurrent motor movement or vocalization.

**AND**

B. Extreme limitation of one, or marked limitation of two, of the following areas of mental functioning (see 12.00F):

1. Understand, remember, or apply information (see 12.00E1).

2. Interact with others (see 12.00E2).

3. Concentrate, persist, or maintain pace (see 12.00E3).

4. Adapt or manage oneself (see 12.00E4).

12.12 [Reserved]
12.13 Eating disorders (see 12.00B10), satisfied by A and B:

A. Medical documentation of a persistent alteration in eating or eating-related behavior that results in a change in consumption or absorption of food and that significantly impairs physical or psychological health.

**AND**

B. Extreme limitation of one, or marked limitation of two, of the following areas of mental functioning (see 12.00F):

1. Understand, remember, or apply information (see 12.00E1).

2. Interact with others (see 12.00E2).

3. Concentrate, persist, or maintain pace (see 12.00E3).

4. Adapt or manage oneself (see 12.00E4).

12.15 Trauma- and stressor-related disorders (see 12.00B11), satisfied by A and B, or A and C:

A. Medical documentation of *all* of the following:

1. Exposure to actual or threatened death, serious injury, or violence;

2. Subsequent involuntary re-experiencing of the traumatic event (for example, intrusive memories, dreams, or flashbacks);

3. Avoidance of external reminders of the event;

4. Disturbance in mood and behavior; and

5. Increases in arousal and reactivity (for example, exaggerated startle response, sleep disturbance).

**AND**

B. Extreme limitation of one, or marked limitation of two, of the following areas of mental functioning (see 12.00F):

1. Understand, remember, or apply information (see 12.00E1).

2. Interact with others (see 12.00E2).

3. Concentrate, persist, or maintain pace (see 12.00E3).

4. Adapt or manage oneself (see 12.00E4).

**OR**
C. Your mental disorder in this listing category is "serious and persistent;" that is, you have a medically documented history of the existence of the disorder over a period of at least 2 years, and there is evidence of both:

*1.* Medical treatment, mental health therapy, psychosocial support(s), or a highly structured setting(s) that is ongoing and that diminishes the symptoms and signs of your mental disorder (see 12.00G2b); *and*

2. Marginal adjustment, that is, you have minimal capacity to adapt to changes in your environment or to demands that are not already part of your daily life (see 12.00G2c).

13.01 Category of Impairments, Malignant Neoplastic Diseases
*13.02* Soft tissue cancers of the head and neck *(except salivary glands - 13.08 - and thyroid gland - 13.09).*

A. Inoperable or unresectable.

OR
B. Persistent or recurrent disease following initial anticancer therapy, except persistence or recurrence in the true vocal cord.

OR
OR
C. With metastases beyond the regional lymph nodes.

OR
D. Small-cell (oat cell) carcinoma.

OR
E. Soft tissue cancers originating in the head and neck treated with multimodal anticancer therapy (see 13.00E3c). Consider under a disability until at least 18 months from the date of diagnosis. Thereafter, evaluate any residual impairment(s) under the criteria for the affected body system.

*13.03 Skin.*
A. Sarcoma or carcinoma with metastases to or beyond the regional lymph nodes.

OR
B. Carcinoma invading deep extradermal structures (for example, skeletal muscle, cartilage, or bone).

1. Recurrent after wide excision (except an additional primary melanoma at a different site, which is not considered to be recurrent disease).

2. With metastases as described in a, b, or c:

a. Metastases to one or more clinically apparent nodes; that is, nodes that are detected by imaging studies (excluding lymphoscintigraphy) or by clinical examination.

b. If the nodes are not clinically apparent, with metastases to four or more nodes.

c. Metastases to adjacent skin (satellite lesions) or distant sites.

13.04 Soft tissue sarcoma.
A. With regional or distant metastases.

OR
B. Persistent or recurrent following initial anticancer therapy.

13.05 Lymphoma *(including mycosis fungoides, but excluding T-cell lymphoblastic lymphoma - 13.06). (See* 13.00K1 and 13.00K2c.)

A. Non-Hodgkin's lymphoma, as described in 1 or 2:

1. Aggressive lymphoma (including diffuse large B-cell lymphoma) persistent or recurrent following initial anticancer therapy.

2. Indolent lymphoma (including mycosis fungoides and follicular small cleaved cell) requiring initiation of more than one (single mode or multimodal) anticancer treatment regimen within a period of 12 consecutive months. Consider under a disability from at least the date of initiation of the treatment regimen that failed within 12 months.

OR
B. Hodgkin lymphoma with failure to achieve clinically complete remission, or recurrent lymphoma within 12 months of completing initial anticancer therapy.

OR

C. With bone marrow or stem cell transplantation. Consider under a disability until at least 12 months from the date of transplantation. Thereafter, evaluate any residual impairment(s) under the criteria for the affected body system.

OR

D. Mantle cell lymphoma.

13.06 Leukemia. (*See* 13.00K2.)

A. Acute leukemia (including T-cell lymphoblastic lymphoma). Consider under a disability until at least 24 months from the date of diagnosis or relapse, or at least 12 months from the date of bone marrow or stem cell transplantation, whichever is later. Thereafter, evaluate any residual impairment(s) under the criteria for the affected body system.

OR

B. Chronic myelogenous leukemia, as described in 1 or 2:

1. Accelerated or blast phase (see 13.00K2b). Consider under a disability until at least 24 months from the date of diagnosis or relapse, or at least 12 months from the date of bone marrow or stem cell transplantation, whichever is later. Thereafter, evaluate any residual impairment(s) under the criteria for the affected body system.

2. Chronic phase, as described in a or b:

a. Consider under a disability until at least 12 months from the date of bone marrow or stem cell transplantation. Thereafter, evaluate any residual impairment(s) under the criteria for the affected body system.

b. Progressive disease following initial anticancer therapy.

*13.07* Multiple myeloma *(confirmed by appropriate serum or urine protein electrophoresis and bone marrow findings).*

A. Failure to respond or progressive disease following initial anticancer therapy.

OR

B. With bone marrow or stem cell transplantation. Consider under a disability until at least 12 months from the date of transplantation. Thereafter, evaluate any residual impairment(s) under the criteria for the affected body system.

13.08 Salivary glands - carcinoma or sarcoma with metastases beyond the regional lymph nodes.

13.09 Thyroid gland.
A. Anaplastic (undifferentiated) carcinoma.

OR
B. Carcinoma with metastases beyond the regional lymph nodes progressive despite radioactive iodine therapy.

OR
C. Medullary carcinoma with metastases beyond the regional lymph nodes.

13.10 Breast (except sarcoma - 13.04). (*See* 13.00K4.)

A. Locally advanced cancer (inflammatory carcinoma, cancer of any size with direct extension to the chest wall or skin, or cancer of any size with metastases to the ipsilateral internal mammary nodes).

OR
B. Carcinoma with metastases to the supraclavicular or infraclavicular nodes, to 10 or more axillary nodes, or with distant metastases.

OR
C. Recurrent carcinoma, except local recurrence that remits with anticancer therapy.

OR
D. Small-cell (oat cell) carcinoma.

OR
E. With secondary lymphedema that is caused by anticancer therapy and treated by surgery to salvage or restore the functioning of an upper extremity. (See 13.00K4b.) Consider under a disability until at least 12 months from the date of the surgery that treated the secondary lymphedema. Thereafter, evaluate any residual impairment(s) under the criteria for the affected body system.

13.11 *Skeletal system* - sarcoma.
A. Inoperable or unresectable.

OR
B. Recurrent cancer (except local recurrence) after initial anticancer therapy.

OR
C. With distant metastases.

OR

D. All other cancers originating in bone with multimodal anticancer therapy (see 13.00E3c). Consider under a disability for 12 months from the date of diagnosis. Thereafter, evaluate any residual impairment(s) under the criteria for the affected body system.

13.12 Maxilla, orbit, or temporal fossa.
A. Sarcoma or carcinoma of any type with regional or distant metastases.

OR

B. Carcinoma of the antrum with extension into the orbit or ethmoid or sphenoid sinus.

OR

C. Cancer with extension to the orbit, meninges, sinuses, or base of the skull.

13.13 Nervous system. (See 13.00K6.)

A. Primary central nervous system (CNS; that is, brain and spinal cord) cancers, as described in 1, 2, or 3:

1. Glioblastoma multiforme, ependymoblastoma, and diffuse intrinsic brain stem gliomas (see 13.00K6a).

2. Any Grade III or Grade IV CNS cancer (see 13.00K6b), including astrocytomas, sarcomas, and medulloblastoma and other primitive neuroectodermal tumors (PNETs).

3. Any primary CNS cancer, as described in a or b:

a. Metastatic.

b. Progressive or recurrent following initial anticancer therapy.

OR

B. Primary peripheral nerve or spinal root cancers, as described in 1 or 2:

1. Metastatic.

2. Progressive or recurrent following initial anticancer therapy.

13.14 Lungs.
A. Non-small-cell carcinoma - inoperable, unresectable, recurrent, or metastatic disease to or beyond the hilar nodes.

OR

B. Small-cell (oat cell) carcinoma.

OR

C. Carcinoma of the superior sulcus (including Pancoast tumors) with multimodal anticancer therapy (see 13.00E3c). Consider under a disability until at least 18 months from the date of diagnosis. Thereafter, evaluate any residual impairment(s) under the criteria for the affected body system.

13.15 Pleura or mediastinum.

A. Malignant mesothelioma of pleura.

OR

B. Tumors of the mediastinum, as described in 1 or 2:

1. With metastases to or beyond the regional lymph nodes.

2. Persistent or recurrent following initial anticancer therapy.

OR

C. Small-cell (oat cell) carcinoma.

13.16 Esophagus or stomach.
A. Carcinoma or sarcoma of the esophagus.

OR

B. Carcinoma or sarcoma of the stomach, as described in 1 or 2:

1. Inoperable, unresectable, extending to surrounding structures, or recurrent.

2. With metastases to or beyond the regional lymph nodes.

OR

C. Small-cell (oat cell) carcinoma.

13.17 Small intestine - carcinoma, sarcoma, or carcinoid.

A. Inoperable, unresectable, or recurrent.

OR

B. With metastases beyond the regional lymph nodes.

OR

C. Small-cell (oat cell) carcinoma.

13.18 Large intestine *(from ileocecal valve to and including anal canal).*

A. Adenocarcinoma that is inoperable, unresectable, or recurrent.

OR

B. Squamous cell carcinoma of the anus, recurrent after surgery.

OR
C. With metastases beyond the regional lymph nodes.

OR
D. Small-cell (oat cell) carcinoma.

13.19 Liver or gallbladder - cancer of the liver, gallbladder, or bile ducts.

13.20 Pancreas.
A. Carcinoma (except islet cell carcinoma).

OR
B. Islet cell carcinoma that is physiologically active and is either inoperable or unresectable.

13.21 Kidneys, adrenal glands, or ureters - carcinoma.

A. Inoperable, unresectable, or recurrent.

OR
B. With metastases to or beyond the regional lymph nodes.

13.22 Urinary bladder - carcinoma.

A. With infiltration beyond the bladder wall.

OR
B. Recurrent after total cystectomy.

OR
C. Inoperable or unresectable.

OR
D. With metastases to or beyond the regional lymph nodes.

OR
E. Small-cell (oat cell) carcinoma.

13.23 Cancers of the female genital tract - carcinoma or sarcoma (including primary peritoneal carcinoma).

A. Uterus (corpus), as described in 1, 2, or 3:

1. Invading adjoining organs.

2. With metastases to or beyond the regional lymph nodes.

3. Persistent or recurrent following initial anticancer therapy.

OR

B. Uterine cervix, as described in 1, 2, or 3:

1. Extending to the pelvic wall, lower portion of the vagina, or adjacent or distant organs.

2. Persistent or recurrent following initial anticancer therapy.

3. With metastases to distant (for example, para-aortic or supraclavicular) lymph nodes.

OR

C. Vulva or vagina, as described in 1, 2, or 3:

1. Invading adjoining organs.

2. With metastases to or beyond the regional lymph nodes.

3. Persistent or recurrent following initial anticancer therapy.

OR

D. Fallopian tubes, as described in 1 or 2:

1. Extending to the serosa or beyond.

2. Persistent or recurrent following initial anticancer therapy.

E. Ovaries, as described in 1 or 2:

1. All cancers except germ-cell cancers, with at least one of the following:

a. Extension beyond the pelvis; for example, implants on, or direct extension to, peritoneal, omental, or bowel surfaces.

b. Metastases to or beyond the regional lymph nodes.

c. Recurrent following initial anticancer therapy.

2. Germ-cell cancers - progressive or recurrent following initial anticancer therapy.

OR

F. Small-cell (oat cell) carcinoma.

13.24 Prostate gland - carcinoma.

A. Progressive or recurrent (not including biochemical recurrence) despite initial hormonal intervention. (See 13.00K8.)

OR

B. With visceral metastases (metastases to internal organs).

OR

C. Small cell (oat cell) carcinoma.

13.25 Testicles - cancer with metastatic disease progressive or recurrent following initial chemotherapy.

13.26 Penis - carcinoma with metastases to or beyond the regional lymph nodes.

13.27 Primary site unknown after appropriate search for primary - metastatic carcinoma or sarcoma, except for squamous cell carcinoma confined to the neck nodes.

13.28 Cancer treated by bone marrow or stem cell transplantation. (See 13.00L.)

A. Allogeneic transplantation. Consider under a disability until at least 12 months from the date of transplantation. Thereafter, evaluate any residual impairment(s) under the criteria for the affected body system.

OR

B. Autologous transplantation. Consider under a disability until at least 12 months from the date of the first treatment under the treatment plan that includes transplantation. Thereafter, evaluate any residual impairment(s) under the criteria for the affected body system.

13.29 Malignant melanoma (including skin, ocular, or mucosal melanomas), as described in either A, B, or C:

A. Recurrent (except an additional primary melanoma at a different site, which is not considered to be recurrent disease) following either 1 or 2:

1. Wide excision (skin melanoma).

2. Enucleation of the eye (ocular melanoma).

OR

B. With metastases as described in 1, 2, or 3:

1. Metastases to one or more clinically apparent nodes; that is, nodes that are detected by imaging studies (excluding lymphoscintigraphy) or by clinical

evaluation (palpable).

2. If the nodes are not clinically apparent, with metastases to four or more nodes.

3. Metastases to adjacent skin (satellite lesions) or distant sites (for example, liver, lung, or brain).

OR
C. Mucosal melanoma.

14.01 Category of Impairments, Immune System Disorders.
14.02 Systemic lupus erythematosus. As described in 14.00D1. With:

A. Involvement of two or more organs/body systems, with:

1. One of the organs/body systems involved to at least a moderate level of severity; and

2. At least two of the constitutional symptoms or signs (severe fatigue, fever, malaise, or involuntary weight loss).

or
B. Repeated manifestations of SLE, with at least two of the constitutional symptoms or signs (severe fatigue, fever, malaise, or involuntary weight loss) and one of the following at the marked level:

1. Limitation of activities of daily living.

2. Limitation in maintaining social functioning.

3. Limitation in completing tasks in a timely manner due to deficiencies in concentration, persistence, or pace.

14.03 Systemic vasculitis. As described in 14.00D2. With:

A. Involvement of two or more organs/body systems, with:

1. One of the organs/body systems involved to at least a moderate level of severity; and

2. At least two of the constitutional symptoms or signs (severe fatigue, fever, malaise, or involuntary weight loss).

or
B. Repeated manifestations of systemic vasculitis, with at least two of the constitutional symptoms or signs (severe fatigue, fever, malaise, or involuntary

weight loss) and one of the following at the marked level:

1. Limitation of activities of daily living.

2. Limitation in maintaining social functioning.

3. Limitation in completing tasks in a timely manner due to deficiencies in concentration, persistence, or pace.

14.04 Systemic sclerosis (scleroderma). As described in 14.00D3. With:

A. Involvement of two or more organs/body systems, with:

1. One of the organs/body systems involved to at least a moderate level of severity; and

2. At least two of the constitutional symptoms or signs (severe fatigue, fever, malaise, or involuntary weight loss).

or
B. With one of the following:

1. Toe contractures or fixed deformity of one or both feet, resulting in the inability to ambulate effectively as defined in 14.00C6; or

2. Finger contractures or fixed deformity in both hands, resulting in the inability to perform fine and gross movements effectively as defined in 14.00C7; or

3. Atrophy with irreversible damage in one or both lower extremities, resulting in the inability to ambulate effectively as defined in 14.00C6; or

4. Atrophy with irreversible damage in both upper extremities, resulting in the inability to perform fine and gross movements effectively as defined in 14.00C7.

or
C. Raynaud's phenomenon, characterized by:

1. Gangrene involving at least two extremities; or

2. Ischemia with ulcerations of toes or fingers, resulting in the inability to ambulate effectively or to perform fine and gross movements effectively as defined in 14.00C6 and 14.00C7;

or
D. Repeated manifestations of systemic sclerosis (scleroderma), with at least two of the constitutional symptoms or signs (severe fatigue, fever, malaise, or

138

involuntary weight loss) and one of the following at the marked level:

1. Limitation of activities of daily living.

2. Limitation in maintaining social functioning.

3. Limitation in completing tasks in a timely manner due to deficiencies in concentration, persistence, or pace.

14.05 Polymyositis and dermatomyositis. As described in 14.00D4. With:

A. Proximal limb-girdle (pelvic or shoulder) muscle weakness, resulting in inability to ambulate effectively or inability to perform fine and gross movements effectively as defined in 14.00C6 and 14.00C7.

or
B. Impaired swallowing (dysphagia) with aspiration due to muscle weakness.

or
C. Impaired respiration due to intercostal and diaphragmatic muscle weakness.

or
D. Diffuse calcinosis with limitation of joint mobility or intestinal motility.

or
E. Repeated manifestations of polymyositis or dermatomyositis, with at least two of the constitutional symptoms or signs (severe fatigue, fever, malaise, or involuntary weight loss) and one of the following at the marked level:

1. Limitation of activities of daily living.

2. Limitation in maintaining social functioning.

3. Limitation in completing tasks in a timely manner due to deficiencies in concentration, persistence, or pace.

14.06 Undifferentiated and mixed connective tissue disease. As described in 14.00D5. With:

A. Involvement of two or more organs/body systems, with:

1. One of the organs/body systems involved to at least a moderate level of severity; and

2. At least two of the constitutional symptoms or signs (severe fatigue, fever, malaise, or involuntary weight loss).

or

B. Repeated manifestations of undifferentiated or mixed connective tissue disease, with at least two of the constitutional symptoms or signs (severe fatigue, fever, malaise, or involuntary weight loss) and one of the following at the marked level:

1. Limitation of activities of daily living.

2. Limitation in maintaining social functioning.

3. Limitation in completing tasks in a timely manner due to deficiencies in concentration, persistence, or pace.

14.07 Immune deficiency disorders, excluding HIV infection. As described in 14.00E. With:

A. One or more of the following infections. The infection(s) must either be resistant to treatment or require hospitalization or intravenous treatment three or more times in a 12-month period.

1. Sepsis; or

2. Meningitis; or

3. Pneumonia; or

4. Septic arthritis; or

5. Endocarditis; or

6. Sinusitis documented by appropriate medically acceptable imaging.

or

B. Stem cell transplantation as described under 14.00E3. Consider under a disability until at least 12 months from the date of transplantation. Thereafter, evaluate any residual impairment(s) under the criteria for the affected body system.

or

C. Repeated manifestations of an immune deficiency disorder, with at least two of the constitutional symptoms or signs (severe fatigue, fever, malaise, or involuntary weight loss) and one of the following at the marked level:

1. Limitation of activities of daily living.

2. Limitation in maintaining social function.

3. Limitation in completing tasks in a timely manner due to deficiencies in concentration, persistence, or pace.

14.08 [Reserved]

14.09 Inflammatory arthritis. As described in 14.00D6. With:

A. Persistent inflammation or persistent deformity of:

1. One or more major peripheral weight-bearing joints resulting in the inability to ambulate effectively (as defined in 14.00C6); or

2. One or more major peripheral joints in each upper extremity resulting in the inability to perform fine and gross movements effectively (as defined in 14.00C7).

or

B. Inflammation or deformity in one or more major peripheral joints with:

1. Involvement of two or more organs/body systems with one of the organs/body systems involved to at least a moderate level of severity; and

2. At least two of the constitutional symptoms or signs (severe fatigue, fever, malaise, or involuntary weight loss).

or

C. Ankylosing spondylitis or other spondyloarthropathies, with:

1. Ankylosis (fixation) of the dorsolumbar or cervical spine as shown by appropriate medically acceptable imaging and measured on physical examination at 45° or more of flexion from the vertical position (zero degrees); or

2. Ankylosis (fixation) of the dorsolumbar or cervical spine as shown by appropriate medically acceptable imaging and measured on physical examination at 30° or more of flexion (but less than 45°) measured from the vertical position (zero degrees), and involvement of two or more organs/body systems with one of the organs/body systems involved to at least a moderate level of severity.

or

D. Repeated manifestations of inflammatory arthritis, with at least two of the constitutional symptoms or signs (severe fatigue, fever, malaise, or involuntary weight loss) and one of the following at the marked level:

1. Limitation of activities of daily living.

2. Limitation in maintaining social functioning.

3. Limitation in completing tasks in a timely manner due to deficiencies in concentration, persistence, or pace.

14.10 Sjögren's syndrome. As described in 14.00D7. With:

A. Involvement of two or more organs/body systems, with:

1. One of the organs/body systems involved to at least a moderate level of severity; and

2. At least two of the constitutional symptoms or signs (severe fatigue, fever, malaise, or involuntary weight loss).

or
B. Repeated manifestations of Sjögren's syndrome, with at least two of the constitutional symptoms or signs (severe fatigue, fever, malaise, or involuntary weight loss) and one of the following at the marked level:

1. Limitation of activities of daily living.

2. Limitation in maintaining social functioning.

3. Limitation in completing tasks in a timely manner due to deficiencies in concentration, persistence, or pace.

14.11 Human immunodeficiency virus (HIV) infection. With documentation as described in 14.00F1 and one of the following:

A. Multicentric (not localized or unicentric) Castleman disease affecting multiple groups of lymph nodes or organs containing lymphoid tissue (see 14.00F3a).

OR
B. Primary central nervous system lymphoma (see 14.00F3b).

OR
C. Primary effusion lymphoma (see 14.00F3c).

OR
D. Progressive multifocal leukoencephalopathy (see 14.00F3d).

OR
E. Pulmonary Kaposi sarcoma (see 14.00F3e).

OR

F. Absolute CD4 count of 50 cells/mm 3 or less (see 14.00F4).

OR

G. Absolute CD4 count of less than 200 cells/mm 3 or CD4 percentage of less than 14 percent, *and* one of the following (values do not have to be measured on the same date) (see 14.00F5):

1. BMI measurement of less than 18.5; or

2. Hemoglobin measurement of less than 8.0 grams per deciliter (g/dL).

OR

H. Complication(s) of HIV infection requiring at least three hospitalizations within a 12-month period and at least 30 days apart (see 14.00F6). Each hospitalization must last at least 48 hours, including hours in a hospital emergency department immediately before the hospitalization.

OR

I. Repeated (as defined in 14.00I3) manifestations of HIV infection, including those listed in 14.11A-H, but without the requisite findings for those listings (for example, Kaposi sarcoma not meeting the criteria in 14.11E), or other manifestations (including, but not limited to, cardiovascular disease (including myocarditis, pericardial effusion, pericarditis, endocarditis, or pulmonary arteritis), diarrhea, distal sensory polyneuropathy, glucose intolerance, gynecologic conditions (including cervical cancer or pelvic inflammatory disease, see 14.00F7), hepatitis, HIV-associated dementia, immune reconstitution inflammatory syndrome (IRIS), infections (bacterial, fungal, parasitic, or viral), lipodystrophy (lipoatrophy or lipohypertrophy), malnutrition, muscle weakness, myositis, neurocognitive or other mental limitations not meeting the criteria in 12.00, oral hairy leukoplakia, osteoporosis, pancreatitis, peripheral neuropathy) resulting in significant, documented symptoms or signs (for example, but not limited to, fever, headaches, insomnia, involuntary weight loss, malaise, nausea, night sweats, pain, severe fatigue, or vomiting) and one of the following at the marked level:

1. Limitation of activities of daily living.

2. Limitation in maintaining social functioning.

3. Limitation in completing tasks in a timely manner due to deficiencies in concentration, persistence, or pace.

# APPENDIX 2: IMPAIRMENTS THAT QUALIFY FOR THE COMPASSIONATE ALLOWANCES PROGRAM

1. Acute Leukemia
2. Adrenal Cancer - with distant metastases or inoperable, unresectable or recurrent
3. Adult Non-Hodgkin Lymphoma
4. Adult Onset Huntington Disease
5. Aicardi-Goutieres Syndrome
6. Alexander Disease (ALX) - Neonatal and Infantile
7. Allan-Herndon-Dudley Syndrome

8. Alobar Holoprosencephaly
9. Alpers Disease
10. Alpha Mannosidosis - Type II and III
11. ALS/Parkinsonism Dementia Complex
12. Alstrom Syndrome
13. Alveolar Soft Part Sarcoma
14. Amegakaryocytic Thrombocytopenia
15. Amyotrophic Lateral Sclerosis (ALS)
16. Anaplastic Adrenal Cancer - Adult with distant metastases or inoperable, unresectable or recurrent
17. Angelman Syndrome
18. Angiosarcoma
19. Aortic Atresia
20. Aplastic Anemia
21. Astrocytoma - Grade III and IV
22. Ataxia Telangiectasia

23. Atypical Teratoid/Rhabdoid Tumor
24. Batten Disease
25. Beta Thalassemia Major
26. Bilateral Optic Atrophy- Infantile
27. Bilateral Retinoblastoma
28. Bladder Cancer - with distant metastases or inoperable or unresectable
29. Breast Cancer - with distant metastases or inoperable or unresectable
30. Canavan Disease (CD)
31. CACH--Vanishing White Matter Disease-Infantile and Childhood Onset Forms (Effective 9/16/2017)
32. Carcinoma of Unknown Primary Site
33. Cardiac Amyloidosis- AL Type

34. Caudal Regression Syndrome - Types III and IV
35. Cerebro Oculo Facio Skeletal (COFS) Syndrome
36. Cerebrotendinous Xanthomatosis
37. Child Lymphoblastic Lymphoma
38. Child Lymphoma
39. Child Neuroblastoma - with distant metastases or recurrent
40. Chondrosarcoma - with multimodal therapy
41. Chronic Idiopathic Intestinal Pseudo Obstruction
42. Chronic Myelogenous Leukemia (CML) - Blast Phase
43. Coffin-Lowry Syndrome
44. Congenital Lymphedema
45. Congenital Myotonic Dystrophy (Effective 9/16/2017)
46. Cornelia de Lange Syndrome - Classic Form
47. Corticobasal Degeneration
48. Creutzfeldt-Jakob Disease (CJD) – Adult
49. Cri du Chat Syndrome
50. Degos Disease - Systemic
51. DeSanctis Cacchione Syndrome

52. Dravet Syndrome
53. Early-Onset Alzheimer's Disease
54. Edwards Syndrome (Trisomy 18)
55. Eisenmenger Syndrome
56. Endometrial Stromal Sarcoma
57. Endomyocardial Fibrosis
58. Ependymoblastoma (Child Brain Cancer)
59. Erdheim Chester Disease
60. Esophageal Cancer
61. Esthesioneuroblastoma
62. Ewing Sarcoma
63. Farber Disease (FD) – Infantile
64. Fatal Familial Insomnia
65. Fibrodysplasia Ossificans Progressiva
66. Follicular Dendritic Cell Sarcoma - metastatic or recurrent
67. Friedreichs Ataxia (FRDA)
68. Frontotemporal Dementia (FTD), Picks Disease -Type A – Adult
69. Fryns Syndrome
70. Fucosidosis - Type 1
71. Fukuyama Congenital Muscular Dystrophy
72. Fulminant Giant Cell Myocarditis
73. Galactosialidosis - Early and Late Infantile Types
74. Gallbladder Cancer
75. Gaucher Disease (GD) - Type 2
76. Giant Axonal Neuropathy
77. Glioblastoma Multiforme (Brain Cancer)
78. Glioma Grade III and IV
79. Glutaric Acidemia - Type II
80. Head and Neck Cancers - with distant metastasis or inoperable or unresectable
81. Heart Transplant Graft Failure
82. Heart Transplant Wait List - 1A/1B

83. Hemophagocytic Lymphohistiocytosis (HLH) - Familial Type
84. Hepatoblastoma
85. Hepatopulmonary Syndrome
86. Hepatorenal Syndrome
87. Histiocytosis Syndromes
88. Hoyeaal-Hreidarsson Syndrome
89. Hutchinson-Gilford Progeria Syndrome

90. Hydranencephaly
91. Hypocomplementemic Urticarial Vasculitis Syndrome
92. Hypophosphatasia Perinatal (Lethal) and Infantile Onset Types
93. Hypoplastic Left Heart Syndrome
94. I Cell Disease
95. Idiopathic Pulmonary Fibrosis
96. Infantile Free Sialic Acid Storage Disease
97. Infantile Neuroaxonal Dystrophy (INAD)
98. Infantile Neuronal Ceroid Lipofuscinoses
99. Inflammatory Breast Cancer (IBC)

100. Intracranial Hemangiopericytoma
101. Jervell and Lange-Nielsen Syndrome
102. Joubert Syndrome
103. Junctional Epidermolysis Bullosa - Lethal Type
104. Juvenile Onset Huntington Disease
105. Kidney Cancer - inoperable or unresectable
106. Kleefstra Syndrome (Effective 9/16/2017)
107. Krabbe Disease (KD) – Infantile
108. Kufs Disease - Type A and B
109. Large Intestine Cancer - with distant metastasis or not operable, unresectable or recurrent
110. Late Infantile Neuronal Ceroid Lipofuscinoses
111. Leigh's Disease

112. Leiomyosarcoma
113. Leptomeningeal Carcinomatosis
114. Lesch-Nyhan Syndrome (LNS)
115. Lewy Body Dementia
116. Liposarcoma - metastatic or recurrent
117. Lissencephaly
118. Liver Cancer
119. Lowe Syndrome
120. Lymphomatoid Granulomatosis - Grade III
121. Malignant Brain Stem Gliomas – Childhood
122. Malignant Ectomesenchymoma
123. Malignant Gastrointestinal Stromal Tumor
124. Malignant Germ Cell Tumor
125. Malignant Multiple Sclerosis
126. Malignant Renal Rhabdoid Tumor
127. Mantle Cell Lymphoma (MCL)
128. Maple Syrup Urine Disease
129. Marshall-Smith Syndrome
130. Mastocytosis - Type IV
131. MECP2 Duplication Syndrome
132. Medulloblastoma - with metastases
133. Menkes Disease - Classic or Infantile Onset Form
134. Merkel Cell Carcinoma - with metastases
135. Merosin Deficient Congenital Muscular Dystrophy
136. Metachromatic Leukodystrophy (MLD) - Late Infantile
137. Mitral Valve Atresia
138. Mixed Dementias
139. MPS I, formerly known as Hurler Syndrome
140. MPS II, formerly known as Hunter Syndrome
141. MPS III, formerly known as Sanfilippo Syndrome
142. Mucosal Malignant Melanoma
143. Multicentric Castleman Disease
144. Multiple System Atrophy
145. Myoclonic Epilepsy with Ragged Red Fibers

Syndrome
146. Neonatal Adrenoleukodystrophy
147. Nephrogenic Systemic Fibrosis
148. Neurodegeneration with Brain Iron Accumulation - Types 1 and 2
149. NFU-1 Mitochondrial Disease

150. Niemann-Pick Disease (NPD) - Type A
151. Niemann-Pick Disease-Type C
152. Nonketotic Hyperglycinemia
153. Non-Small Cell Lung Cancer
154. Obliterative Bronchiolitis
155. Ohtahara Syndrome
156. Oligodendroglioma Brain Cancer- Grade III
157. Ornithine Transcarbamylase (OTC) Deficiency
158. Orthochromatic Leukodystrophy with Pigmented Glia
159. Osteogenesis Imperfecta (OI) - Type II
160. Osteosarcoma, formerly known as Bone Cancer - with distant metastases or inoperable or unresectable

161. Ovarian Cancer – with distant metastases or inoperable or nresectable
162. Pallister-Killian Syndrome
163. Pancreatic Cancer
164. Paraneoplastic Pemphigus
165. Patau Syndrome (Trisomy 13)
166. Pearson Syndrome
167. Pelizaeus-Merzbacher Disease-Classic Form
168. Pelizaeus-Merzbacher Disease-Connatal Form
169. Peripheral Nerve Cancer - metastatic or recurrent
170. Peritoneal Mesothelioma
171. Peritoneal Mucinous Carcinomatosis
172. Perry Syndrome
173. Phelan-McDermid Syndrome

174. Pleural Mesothelioma
175. Pompe Disease – Infantile
176. Primary Central Nervous System Lymphoma
177. Primary Effusion Lymphoma
178. Primary Progressive Aphasia
179. Progressive Bulbar Palsy
180. Progressive Multifocal Leukoencephalopathy
181. Progressive Supranuclear Palsy
182. Prostate Cancer - Hormone Refractory Disease – or with visceral metastases
183. Pulmonary Atresia
184. Pulmonary Kaposi Sarcoma
185. Retinopathy of Prematurity - Stage V
186. Rett (RTT) Syndrome
187. Revesz Syndrome
188. Rhabdomyosarcoma
189. Rhizomelic Chondrodysplasia Punctata
190. Roberts Syndrome
191. Salivary Cancers
192. Sandhoff Disease
193. Schindler Disease - Type 1
194. Seckel Syndrome
195. Severe Combined Immunodeficiency - Childhood
196. Single Ventricle
197. Sinonasal Cancer
198. Sjogren-Larsson Syndrome
199. Skin Malignant Melanoma with Metastases
200. Small Cell Cancer (Large Intestine, Prostate or Thymus)
201. Small Cell Cancer of the Female Genital Tract
202. Small Cell Lung Cancer
203. Small Intestine Cancer - with distant metastases or inoperable, nresectable or recurrent
204. Smith Lemli Opitz Syndrome

205. Soft Tissue Sarcoma - with distant metastases or recurrent

206. Spinal Muscular Atrophy (SMA) - Types 0 and 1
207. Spinal Nerve Root Cancer-metastatic or recurrent
208. Spinocerebellar Ataxia
209. Stiff Person Syndrome
210. Stomach Cancer - with distant metastases or inoperable, unresectable or recurrent
211. Subacute Sclerosing Panencephalitis
212. Tabes Dorsalis
213. Tay Sachs Disease - Infantile Type
214. Thanatophoric Dysplasia - Type 1
215. Thyroid Cancer
216. Transplant Coronary Artery Vasculopathy
217. Tricuspid Atresia
218. Ullrich Congenital Muscular Dystrophy
219. Ureter Cancer - with distant metastases or inoperable, unresectable or recurrent
220. Usher Syndrome - Type I
221. Ventricular Assist Device Recipient - Left, Right, or Biventricular
222. Walker Warburg Syndrome
223. Wolf-Hirschhorn Syndrome
224. Wolman Disease
225. X-Linked Lymphoproliferative Disease
226. X-Linked Myotubular Myopathy
227. Xeroderma Pigmentosum
228. Zellweger Syndrome

# APPENDIX 3: SAMPLE FORMS FOR TREATING DOCTORS

Form 1: Physical Residual Functional Capacity Assessment
Name:
SSN:
DOB:
Date:

(1)    Please list your patient's diagnoses:

(2)    Please circle how much your patient is able to lift
Less than 10lbs
10lbs
15-20lbs
Over 20 lbs

(3)    Please circle how long your patient can walk at one time
Less than 15 mins
15-30 mins
30-45 mins
Over 45 mins

(4)    Have you prescribed an assistive device for your patient (i.e. cane, walker, etc.)?

(5)    Please circle how long your patient can stand at one time
Less than 15 mins
15-30 mins
30-45 mins
Over 45 mins

(6)    Please circle how long your patient can sit at one time without interruption
Less than 15 mins
15-30 mins
30-45 mins

45 – 60 mins
Over 60 mins

    (7)   Does your patient need to elevate his or her legs at or above waist level during the day?

    (8)   Does your patient need to change positions? If yes, please circle how often:
More often than every 30 mins
Every 30 mins
Every hour
Every 2 hours

    (9)   (Please circle) Does your patient have the ability to:
Bend: never, occasionally, frequently
Stoop: never, occasionally, frequently
Crawl: never, occasionally, frequently
Squat: never, occasionally, frequently
No useful ability to perform any of the above

    (10)  Is your patient limited in his/her ability to reach overhead?
If yes, please circle: never, occasionally, frequently

    (11)  Is your patient limited in his/her ability to push and pull?
If yes, please circle: never, occasionally, frequently

    (12)  Have you prescribed medications?
    (13)  Please list those medications:

    (14)  What, if any, side effects does your patient experience:

    (15)  Does your patient have the ability to perform work 8 hours a day, 5 days a week?

    (16)  Would your patient require unscheduled breaks during the work day?
How often?
How long would each break last?
Why would your patient need these breaks?

153

(17) Would your patient miss work an excess of 1 day per week?

(18) Have you advised your patient to return to work?

(19) What restrictions and limitations have you given your patient?

Doctor's Signature:
Printed name:
Date:

# Form 2: Psychological Residual Functional Capacity Assessment

Name:

SSN:

DOB:

Date:

*Section 1*

  (1)  Date Patient first seen:

  (2)  Frequency of Contact:

  (3)  Current Diagnosis:                    Axis I:

Axis  II:

Axis III:

Axis IV:

Axis V:

  (4)  Highest GAF in the past year:

  (5)  Describe the patient's course of treatment:

  (6)  Does that patient's psychiatric impairment exacerbate your patient's pain or any other physical symptoms?

  (7)  Please check all signs and symptoms that apply:

___  Anhedonia or pervasive loss of interest in almost all activities

___  Appetite disturbance with weight change

___  Apprehensive expectation

___  Autonomic hyperactivity

___  Bipolar syndrome with a history of episodic periods manifested by the full symptomatic picture of both manic and depressive syndromes (and currently characterized by either or both syndromes)

___  Blunt, flat or inappropriate affect

___  Catatonic or other grossly disorganized behavior

___  Change in personality

___  Decreased energy

___  Decreased need for sleep

___  Deeply ingrained, maladaptive patterns of behavior

___  Difficulty thinking or concentrating

___  Disorientation to time and place

___  Easy distractability

___  Emotional lability

155

___ Emotional withdrawal or isolation

___ Feelings of guilt or worthlessness

___ Flight of ideas

___ Generalized persistent anxiety

___ Hallucinations or delusions

___ History of multiple physical symptoms of several years duration beginning before age 30, that have caused the individual to take medicine frequently, see a physician often and alter life patterns significantly

___ Hyperactivity

___ Illogical thinking

___ Impairment in impulse control

___ Incoherence

___ Inflated self-esteem

___ Intense and unstable interpersonal relationships and impulsive and damaging behavior

___ Involvement in activities that have a high probability of painful consequences which are not recognized

___ Loosening of associations

___ Loss of intellectual ability of 15 IQ points or more

___ Manic syndrome

___ Memory impairment -- short, intermediate or long term

___ Mood disturbance

___ Motor tension

___ Oddities of thought, perception, speech or behavior

___ Other physical impairments:

___ Paranoid thinking or inappropriate suspiciousness

___ Pathological dependence, passivity or agressivity

___ Pathologically inappropriate suspiciousness or hostility

___ Perceptual or thinking disturbances

___ Persistent disturbances of mood or affect

___ Persistent irrational fear of a specific object, activity, or situation which results in a compelling desire to avoid the dreaded object, activity or situation

___ Persistent non-organic disturbance of vision, speech, hearing, use of a limb, movement and its control, or sensation

___ Poverty of content of speech

___ Pressures of speech

___ Psychological or behavioral abnormalities associated with a dysfunction of the brain with a specific organic factor judged to be etiologically related to the abnormal mental state and loss of previously acquired functional abilities

___ Psychomotor agitation or retardation

___ Recurrent and intrusive recollections of a traumatic experience, which are a source of marked distress

___ Recurrent obsessions or compulsions which are a source of marked distress

___ Recurrent severe panic attacks manifested by a sudden unpredictable onset of intense apprehension, fear, terror and sense of impending doom occurring on the average of at least once per week

___ Seclusiveness or autistic thinking

___ Sleep disturbance

___ Somatization unexplained by organic disturbance

___ Substance dependence

___ Thoughts of suicide

___ Unrealistic interpretation of physical signs or sensations associated with the preoccupation or belief that one has a serious disease or injury

___ Vigilance and scanning

(8) Are your patient's impairments reasonably consistent with the symptoms and functional limitations described in this questionnaire?

## Section 2

Please assess your patient's ability to sustain the following mental activities, during a normal work day, 8 hours per day, 5 days per week. Please use these definitions for the questions below:

Not Significantly Limited: The patient has no limitations or minimal limitations.

Mildly Limited: The patient has some mild limitation in this area but the individual can generally function well.

Moderately Limited: The patient has moderate limitation in this area but the individual is still able to function satisfactorily.

Markedly Limited: The patient has serious limitation in this area. There is substantial loss in the ability to effectively function.

Extremely Limited: The patient has major limitation in this area. There is no useful ability to function in this area.

## A. Understanding and Memory

(1) The ability to remember locations and work-like procedures

___Not significantly Limited
___Mildly Limited
___Moderately Limited
___Markedly Limited
___Extremely Limited

(2) The ability to understand and remember very short and simple instructions

___Not significantly Limited
___Mildly Limited
___Moderately Limited
___Markedly Limited
___Extremely Limited

(3) The ability to understand and remember detailed instructions

___Not significantly Limited
___Mildly Limited
___Moderately Limited
___Markedly Limited
___Extremely Limited

## B. Sustained Concentration and Persistence

(4) The ability to carry out very short and simple instructions.

___Not significantly Limited
___Mildly Limited
___Moderately Limited
___Markedly Limited

___Extremely Limited

   (5)   The ability to carry out detailed instructions.
___Not significantly Limited
___Mildly Limited
___Moderately Limited
___Markedly Limited
___Extremely Limited

   (6)   The ability to maintain attention and concentration for extended periods.
___Not significantly Limited
___Mildly Limited
___Moderately Limited
___Markedly Limited
___Extremely Limited

   (7)   The ability to maintain attention and concentration for extended periods.
___Not significantly Limited
___Mildly Limited
___Moderately Limited
___Markedly Limited
___Extremely Limited

   (8)   The ability to sustain an ordinary routine without special supervision.
___Not significantly Limited
___Mildly Limited
___Moderately Limited
___Markedly Limited
___Extremely Limited

   (9)   The ability to work in coordination with or proximity to others without being distracted by them.
___Not significantly Limited
___Mildly Limited
___Moderately Limited
___Markedly Limited

___Extremely Limited

(10) The ability to make simple work-related decisions.
___Not significantly Limited
___Mildly Limited
___Moderately Limited
___Markedly Limited
___Extremely Limited

(11) The ability to complete a normal work-day and work-week, without interruptions from psychologically-based symptoms and to perform at a consistent pace without an unreasonable number and length of rest periods.
___Not significantly Limited
___Mildly Limited
___Moderately Limited
___Markedly Limited
___Extremely Limited

## C.  Social Interaction

(12) The ability to interact appropriately with the general public.
___Not significantly Limited
___Mildly Limited
___Moderately Limited
___Markedly Limited
___Extremely Limited

(13) The ability to ask simple questions or request assistance.
___Not significantly Limited
___Mildly Limited
___Moderately Limited
___Markedly Limited
___Extremely Limited

(14) The ability to accept instructions and respond appropriately to criticism from supervisors.
___Not significantly Limited
___Mildly Limited

___Moderately Limited
___Markedly Limited
___Extremely Limited

    (15) The ability to get along with coworkers or peers without distracting them or exhibiting behavioral extremes.

___Not significantly Limited
___Mildly Limited
___Moderately Limited
___Markedly Limited
___Extremely Limited

    (16) The ability to get along with coworkers or peers without distracting them or exhibiting behavioral extremes.

___Not significantly Limited
___Mildly Limited
___Moderately Limited
___Markedly Limited
___Extremely Limited

## D. Adaptation

    (17) The ability to respond appropriately to changes in the work setting.

___Not significantly Limited
___Mildly Limited
___Moderately Limited
___Markedly Limited
___Extremely Limited

    (18) The ability to be aware of normal hazards and take appropriate precautions.

___Not significantly Limited
___Mildly Limited
___Moderately Limited
___Markedly Limited
___Extremely Limited

    (19) The ability to travel in unfamiliar places or use public

transportation.
\_\_\_Not significantly Limited
\_\_\_Mildly Limited
\_\_\_Moderately Limited
\_\_\_Markedly Limited
\_\_\_Extremely Limited

(20) The ability to set realistic goals or make plans independently of others.
\_\_\_Not significantly Limited
\_\_\_Mildly Limited
\_\_\_Moderately Limited
\_\_\_Markedly Limited
\_\_\_Extremely Limited

(21) The ability to tolerate stress in a normal work setting.
\_\_\_Not significantly Limited
\_\_\_Mildly Limited
\_\_\_Moderately Limited
\_\_\_Markedly Limited
\_\_\_Extremely Limited

*Section 3*

(1)   Does your patient require *unscheduled* breaks during an 8-hour workday, in addition to the 3 customary breaks (morning, lunch, afternoon)?

If yes, please indicate how many unscheduled breaks will be required, per 2 hour period, the estimated length and reason for the breaks:

(2)   Does your patient have good and bad days?
If yes, please estimate, on average, how many days per month your patient is likely to be absent from work as a result of the impairments, or as a result of necessary medical treatment, such as therapy:

| | | | |
|---|---|---|---|
| \_\_\_ Never | | \_\_\_ 3 days per month | |
| \_\_\_ 1 day per month | | | \_\_\_ 4 days per month |
| \_\_\_ 2 days per month | | | \_\_\_ More than 4 days per |
| month | | | |

(3)    Please describe any additional reasons, not covered above, why your patient would have difficulty working a regular job on a sustained basis.


(4)    Can your patient manage benefits in his / her own best interest?


Doctor's Signature:
Printed name:
Date:

Printed in Great Britain
by Amazon

41116836R00099